GAME OF 2 HALVES

WHY DOESN'T GOD DO SOMETHING?

Grant Smith

Scripture Union, 207–209 Queensway, Bletchley, MK2 2EB, England.

First published 1999

ISBN 1 85999 299 4

British Library Cataloguing-in-Publication Data
A catalogue record for this book is available from the British Library.

Cover design by Viz-A-Viz.
Printed and bound in Great Britain by Cox & Wyman, Reading, Berkshire.

CONTENTS

THE BIT WHERE I SAY THANKS

I've never done this before, so I'm not sure what to say. I've written other books which have never got this far; many people have read them and given me their comments. All those comments, positive or negative, were very useful and contributed towards producing this book. So, thanks.

Somebody who was going to endorse this book asked a friend of ours if she knew what the book was like. She replied, 'I haven't read it, but I know Sue has and I have confidence that Sue will have made sure that the book is safe.' Sue is my wife, of whom you will hear more as you read this book. Without her I would never have written it. Those who know her can't understand why she married me. Although I don't share their disbelief, I can understand where they are coming from. Without Sue I would never have been where I've been, done what I've done, seen what I've seen and kept the friends I've upset. Thanks, Sue.

Grant Smith

FOREWORD

Poverty is boring. We have seen it all too many times. On TV and in magazines, we see pictures of the victims of famine and refugees. And we change the channel or turn the page. It's not because we are mean or selfish. It's just that we have seen those images so often, we don't know what to do with them. There are so many starving people, so many refugees, so many trapped in poverty. What can we do that will really make a difference?

Grant Smith has written a book that could change your world. For a start, you will discover a Christianity that deals with life, not just church. You will meet the real Jesus – not just the one who died and rose again, but the one who also lived on earth with people, helping them, healing them, feeding them, so that they might live as God intended and even choose to follow him themselves. You will understand more of what it means to follow Jesus and be given some practical ways to start working with God to change the world.

Of course, at the end of the day, this is just a book. You can turn the page, just like we do when we see images of poverty. You may even feel quite moved by what you read – then do nothing. Or you may hear Jesus calling you to be closer to him than ever before.

Next time you see the picture of the refugee camp on TV, look a little closer.Don't just look at the crowd – pick out a person, a real person, who has very similar hopes and dreams to you. They have just lost everything. But the same God who loves you loves them, has plans for them, wants to know them and bless them.

Look ever more closely. Somewhere in the picture you will see Jesus. He will be doing what he always does – comforting and encouraging people. But mostly he will be looking at you, asking you to draw near to him as he brings good news to the poor.

This is the Jesus you will find in this book. You will also find real Christianity and a chance to make a real difference.

David Westlake

1 HELLO

I can remember sitting in my maths class at the age of sixteen, right at the back, behind Ian Russell.

Ian was a good friend of mine, until one day my girlfriend decided she fancied Ian more than me, at which point Ian became a bad friend – although, I must confess, it wasn't entirely his fault and, shortly afterwards, he became a good friend again.

Enough of the nostalgia. There were three good reasons for my repeatedly choosing this location in which to study maths.

1 Our teacher had an underrated odour problem which I tried to cast out 'In the name of Jesus' on several occasions but was painfully reminded, every time she raised her right arm to scribe on the blackboard, that I had yet again been unsuccessful.
2 Ian Russell – or Sprout, as his friends affectionately knew him – was an Ironstein in the making. Should any questions come flying in our direction, I felt safe that Sprout would be happy to deflect her penetrating attack and come out with an impressive answer.
3 Ian was a big guy, and I considered that there was a distinct possibility our teacher, Mrs Numbercount, may not even realise I was there. I was therefore able to take cover under my desk, reasonably sure that I would survive the next fifty-five minutes of

life without being dealt an explosive blow by our commandant.

During these times, I can vividly remember contemplating, as I gazed at the back of Sprout's head, *Why does Gwinderlin fancy Ironstein more than me?*

What on earth is the point?

Who really wants to know what the differentiation of x^2 *is anyway? If you integrated after you differentiated, you would come back to where you started,* x^2*.*

Breathtaking stuff, eh?

As a consequence, I used to sit there thinking that it would be far more beneficial if we were taught subjects which had a greater direct application to life, such as Formula One Driving or Parachute Jumping or Disco Dancing. Then I remembered that to teach Disco Dancing, Mrs Numbercount would be raising both arms with far greater regularity than she was currently doing and, unless I could perfect this 'casting out' business, I was probably better off behind Sprout learning differentiation.

Of course, we all know the reality, which is that in order to develop into an adult the full learning process has to be endured. In fact, it has contributed to making me the person I am today. Mrs Numbercount had a vital role to play in my getting an education, passing exams and going on to further studies that eventually led to a job and earning money. However, some deodorant might have eased the process.

In the same way, I believe our overall understanding of the Bible is vital to living the Christian life now while we wait for the life that is to come. The problem, I guess, is that the Bible is so big (although you can get pocket-sized versions). How do we get a grasp of it all?

The subject we are attempting to look at here in this

book, which may not have been apparent so far, is that of concern for the world's poor.

How do we respond to those who are in need?

Do we have a biblical response?

How does what the Bible teaches on caring for the poor fit into the overall framework of being a Christian in our culture, in our time?

The problem with this particular subject is that it is probably not the highest on most people's agenda. I guess we need to ask...

Should it be?

The reason it is probably not at the top of most people's agendas is that it is hardly the most cheery subject in either the Bible or, come to that, life lived without a Bible.

> Preaching the gospel and seeing thousands saved is fun.
>
> Raising people from the dead is impressive.
>
> Taking Bibles to countries that don't allow them is exciting.
>
> Feeding the hungry is depressing as we watch the unfed die.

Let's be honest, concern for the poor is not the most attractive option.

What is our response?

I go round the country, into schools, universities and churches, with a large multimedia show designed to challenge our response to the poor. The show is big-screen video, loud music, smoke, slides, interaction and live presentation. Most people who see it think it is good.

There have been occasions when a church has put on a special Saturday night event to present the show. They have mailed every church in the area, advertised it on the radio, stuck posters all round the town, prayed for months, personally invited the mayor, town-crier and stray dogs. And, on the night, twenty people turn up.

Why?

Well, look at the options for a Saturday night.

Have some friends round, get a pizza and watch a video.

Meet up with some friends, go clubbing and dance the night away.

Go to the pictures, eat popcorn and sit in the back row.

Have a drink, meet up with some mates and eat a kebab on the way home.

Have a nice meal at home and watch TV.

Go and see relatives.

Invite relatives over.

Read a book.

Write a book.

Or...

Go and be faced with the poor around the world, and feel guilty.

Hey, it's a winner every time!

Get real!

The people who organise these events say, 'I don't understand it! Why does nobody want to come?'

Well, I don't understand why they thought *anybody*

would want to come. Let's face it, I wouldn't have been there if it weren't for the fact that I ran the show. (Incidentally, we have stopped doing Saturday night venues, unless it fits into a church's current youth programme.)

What is our response?

We are members of a world club of which there are 5–6 billion participants. God has created the whole lot. He has distributed resources, gifts, talents and opportunity. As time has gone on, some have made more of their opportunities and passed the benefits on to future generations. Others have made less of their opportunities and passed their *dis*benefits on to future generations.

Now let us examine this a little closer.

I live with a partner.

If either my partner or myself falls on hard times, the other supports him/her.

I live with a partner and three children.

If one of these falls on hard times, the others support him/her.

I belong to a church.

If one of the members falls on hard times, the others support him/her.

I belong to a world of God's people.

Millions of them fall on hard times, we all ignore it?

Something has gone wrong!

The trouble is, we don't totally ignore it. We put, in relative terms, a few mites into the collecting tin and think that we are doing what we can. Or we buy a lottery ticket, because that's giving to charity, isn't it?

I was once asked to distribute the little collecting

envelopes for a large charity in my street. There were about fifty homes to distribute to. I figured it wouldn't take long, so I said yes. I dutifully put them through the doors and returned to collect them three days later. From fifty houses, I collected 68p.

The little envelopes and the phone call asking me to do the job cost more than that.

What is our response?

Game of 2 Halves is a Tearfund and Viz-A-Viz project in association with Christians in Sport, which is aimed at raising money for a world in need through sport and young people. It is designed to use what many are already doing every week – playing sport – to help those who would love to play sport but who can't because they are hungry, or because they don't know how to play sport, or because they have no sports facilities.

This project is not simply about buying footballs for Uganda. It is a whole health-and-development programme to give hope to children who have little.

You too can be a part of...

Game of 2 Halves.

2 WHAT IS A CHRISTIAN?

I don't know about you, but I find asking questions a lot easier than answering them. A friend once told me that I never actually answered any questions, I simply replied with another question. Not entirely fair, but then Jesus was persecuted a bit, so why shouldn't I be?

I think this attitude, however, is a consequence of spending time at London Bible College. You see when I went to LBC, I thought that after all that study, and all that research, and all that essay writing, and all that debating, and all that meditation, and all that coffee drinking, I would end up with all the answers. Now, as it happens, I actually think that I *do* have all the answers; it's just unfortunate that people ask all the wrong questions. But then that's human nature for you.

You see, at LBC they asked a lot of questions and they gave several potential answers, but they very rarely told you which one was right. You were left to sort that out for yourself.

For example, I was convinced at one stage of my studies that Jesus was, in fact, a pantomime horse. Now, you give that as an answer to somebody who asks, 'Who is Jesus?', and you ain't going to be taken very seriously, so the best way out is to ask another question.

I go out and about, taking loads of church meetings, and it can be fun. But it can also be tedious, so sometimes I finish and ask the congregation if they have any questions.

I was once at a service where it became obvious there was a member of the congo who felt that the 'gospel' had to be preached at every 'gathering of the saints'. Our dialogue went something like this.

Congo Man: What do you think the purpose of life is?

Me: That's a very big question. Do you want to narrow it down a little?

Congo Man: Yes, OK. Why do you think we are here? *(That helped!)*

Me: What, you mean here in church or here on earth?

Congo Man: Here on earth.

Me: Why do I think *you* are here, or why do I think *I* am here?

Congo Man: Both.

Me: Well, why do *you* think we are here?

Congo Man: I think we are here because... *(etc, etc)*

Me: Good point, but will we ever understand the answer properly?

Congo Man: Probably not.

Me: Any more questions?

By the end of our little session, Congo Man had answered his question and mine. The fact that he got them both wrong, in my opinion, was irrelevant. His answer left him feeling a lot better and me smiling because I had answered nothing.

Life is just one big question

Travelling along the UK's vast network of efficient motorways, I was driving a vehicle in which a fellow worker was passenger, when at great speed I overtook three caravans. Fortunately for them, they all had cars towing them. Obviously, I was not exceeding the speed limit set down by our *God-ordained* government. (A subject for another great book. Not that I am suggesting that *this* is a great book, but there are books around that are great and my next book may well be added to them, rather than this one.)

Anyway, back to the caravans. As we passed them, my travelling companion launched into a whole load of questions about caravans.

Companion:	I don't get it.
Me:	What?
Companion:	Caravans.
Me:	Well, they're cardboard boxes on a pair of wheels.
Companion:	Yeah, I know that. But why do people buy them?
Me:	How do you know people *do* buy them?
Companion:	We just saw three.
Me:	How do you know they weren't aliens driving them?
	(Companion is obviously totally unimpressed by this suggestion.)
Companion:	They are just ridiculous. People fill them up with so many home comforts that, by the time you go on holiday, you have no idea whether you're away or at home.
	(Very good point, I thought.)
	And what an advert for burglars.
Me:	Yes?
Companion:	Fifty weeks of the year this white box

> sits outside your house for the world to see. Then suddenly it's gone. You're hardly going to take it shopping, are you?
>
> *(Good point, I thought.)*
>
> I just don't get it.

You see loads of questions, but what about the answers?

So let me add one more...

What is a Christian?

I used to go to a big Anglican church. When I say big, I mean that both the building and the congregation were big. When I say the congregation was big, I don't mean that individuals were big; what I mean is big numerically. When I say big numerically, I don't mean that the person who recorded how many were in church wrote their figures big; I mean that there were a lot of them.

Got it?

Anyway, back to this big Anglican church. It was just great. It was well-organised. They had services to suit all tastes (though I guess a Muslim would have struggled). There was loads of space for all sorts to take part, from OAPs to children to women to clergy: they could all get a look-in somewhere if they wanted. (Mind you, I don't ever remember doing anything, but I never took it personally.) With all this going on, the services were fast-moving and exciting and challenging and loud – but quiet when required. Just magic.

Even so, I occasionally got bored. My fault, I'm sure – I'm not about to blame the church which worked well for so many good people. Why should I hide behind the church, when it was me who had the problem? I was the one who got bored, not the others.

During these times of momentary backsliding into sin and evil thoughts about the screaming kids who, when told to shut up by their devoted parents, would pull faces at those same devoted parents (who would smile indulgently) and carry on as if to say, *Suckers! Works every time*; I used to ponder, as my concentration was lost by this time! I would sit there and look at all the people and decide which ones were Christians and which ones weren't. Now I know that God is the only one who really knows, but there is no harm in having a guess, is there?

There was the man who welcomed you on the way in – he was probably a Christian. There was the single father who stayed in the service while his child went off to Sparklers – he must be a Christian or he wouldn't stay. There was the woman who did the head count – she must be a Christian. There was the woman with the big hat who sat on the PCC and never talked to anyone other than Important Church People – she was definitely a lady, but as for being a Christian...? No, I don't think so!

There were the two women sitting in front of me, Bertha and Emerald. Emerald – academically OK, listened to a gospel service twenty-three years ago, responded to the appeal, got her own 'Journey into Life', prayed the prayer and made a note in the front of her Bible. Her life, however, carried on totally unaffected by the whole experience.

Now Bertha – a slim active lady – she helps the neighbours and looks after her ageing father (mind you, show me a father of any age who isn't ageing and you're on to a miracle). She arranges the flowers, prays regularly, does 'Daily Notes', although she sometimes misses a day. But she has never really understood the gospel message, never got her own 'Journey into Life', and never prayed the prayer. And no note in the front of the Bible.

So, who's the Christian?

There once was a rich little man called Zack.

Now Zack was a man of power.
Zack was a man of wealth.
Zack was a man of position.
I would guess that Zack was a proud man.

Recently, I was in Kenya. The President of Kenya is a gentleman called Daniel arap Moi.

Moi is a man of power.
Moi is a man of wealth.
Moi is a man of position.
However, Moi is also corrupt.

While I was there, I was travelling through Nairobi. For those of you who have never been there, let me explain that Nairobi, traffic-wise, is very similar to London. The only difference is that you can be driving along a road in three lanes of traffic and suddenly the road disappears. It's not because somebody has stolen it; it's just that the rains and constant traffic have destroyed it, and nobody has thought to repair it, least of all Moi.

So, one day we are in this traffic and everything comes to a halt. There is a policeman on the roundabout and he is stopping all movement. When I say movement, I mean cars, pedestrians, children, dogs, fleas on the dogs... Get the picture?

It's a hot day and our driver is somewhat agitated. We sit there for some five minutes, maybe longer. (It was a bit like those few occasions when somebody important dies and there is a minute's silence.)

After whatever the above period of time was, about twenty motorcycles come racing through. These are policemen (well, the motorcycles were BMWs, the riders were policemen). Following them are a large number of Mercs, all newish, all with one or two people in them, possibly bodyguards or other government officials. Then comes a stretched Merc with Moi sitting in the back. The occasion is Moi going home for lunch. (Actually, I don't know where he was going. But, with the exception of the lunch statement, the rest is all exactly as it happened.)

In my picture of Zack, he might not be on the same level as Moi but he is certainly somewhere near it. We talk of Zack being a tax enforcer and robbing everybody he dealt with. However, I doubt that he would actually lower himself to talk to the common people. He probably had his 'minders' who would make contact with the grubby little taxpayers.

The way the system worked, therefore, was probably a bit like this.

Zack would have his entourage. The traffic would be stopped and a few people would probably lead the way on foot. (They may have had BMWs, but it's not likely.) Then there would have been a few bodyguards on newish donkeys. And then Zack would come through on his stretched donkey. (Obviously, it was stretched because it had to hold this little fat guy up.) Then Zack would direct his tax collectors to go and communicate with the common person and collect the money.

I hope you now have the picture that is in my imagination.

One day Jesus comes to town. What follows is, potentially, the conversation that morning.

Zack comes down to breakfast.

Minders: Morning, Sir Zack.

Zack: Morning.

Minders: Here is your breakfast.

Zack: Yes ... Munch, munch, munch, munch...

Minders: Drool, drool, drool, drool...

Zack: What poor innocent victims have we got on the list for today?

Minders: We don't know if today is going to be a good day for collecting. We think the town might be a bit busy.

Zack: Why?

Minders: A guy called Jesus is coming.

Zack: Look him up in the directory. Does he owe tax?

Minders: We don't think so. He doesn't earn any money.

Zack: So? Neither do the others.

Minders: No, Jesus is a preacher. He saves people and makes sick people well.

Zack: And he's got no money. I should co-co.

Minders: No, he does seem to be straight. Everybody wants to see him.

Zack: OK then, get me a ticket.

Minders: You can't get tickets.

Zack contemplates this situation. The more he contemplates, the more he thinks he would like to meet this oddball. Eventually he orders the motorcade to get ready: 'We will go and see Jesus.'

They go off into town, but don't get very far before traffic grinds to a halt. Zack is confused. Traffic normally stops for him, but now, it seems, there is somebody more important. He gets off the donkey and decides to try and push through the crowd. But he is spotted and today is the day the people get their revenge. There is no way they are going to let the little fat guy through, although he tries several times.

Judging by the noise, Jesus is obviously getting closer. Zack is getting a panic on, thinking he is never going to get to see him. Drastic action is now needed. So he predicts the route Jesus is going to take, then runs on ahead, climbs a tree and waits.

Do you realise what has just happened?

It's like Moi driving through Nairobi, and the traffic is brought to a halt because Billy Graham is coming the other way. So Moi gets out of his stretched Merc and runs to catch a bus, where he climbs up on the top deck and waits for Billy to come through. Just a little unusual.

So there is Zack, up this tree, waiting, and here comes Jesus. Jesus gets to the tree and stops.

Zack can't believe his luck. Not only can he see Jesus, but he actually stops six feet from where Zack is sitting. *Just wait till I tell them this at breakfast in the morning. They will never believe it. I can almost touch Jesus. Oh, this is brilliant!*

Jesus looks up and says, 'Hi, Zack. Get down here. I'm hungry. What about a spot of lunch?'

Confused but amazed, Zack jumps out the tree – well, falls out the tree – and in a moment his status is reinstated.

Zack: Bring the donkeys!

(The crowd reluctantly part, and in come the entourage.)

Zack: Here, Jesus, have a donkey.

Jesus: No, some quiche will be fine.

They go back to Zack's house. Zack gets out the best wine, the best quiche, the best everything. The whole house goes into 'flight of the bumble-bee' mode and food is prepared. They sit down together and the conversation begins.

Meanwhile, the crowd is bemused. They are convinced that Zack is going to be exposed by Jesus for who he really is. So they all go to the house, because this they have got to see. Outside, rumours are spreading – all untrue, but it passes the time. After several hours, Zack appears on his balcony with Jesus standing next to him. Zack stands forward, and it looks as if he is going to address the crowd. The crowd goes silent. All eyes are on the little fat guy. Zack draws breath, there are tears in his eyes, and he says, 'Today I am going to give half of everything to the poor – half my wealth, half my estate, half my stretched donkey. You name it, half goes.

'And – if I have thieved from anybody, I will give back four times what I have stolen.'

This statement does not add up. Thieved from anybody? He thieved from everybody! And Zack is promising to give half of what he's nicked to the poor and pay back four times what he has stolen. Everything he has he has nicked off everybody he has ever met. But he only has half of what he has stolen, so he's three and a half times short of his promise, plus I guess he spent some, too. Zack, in a moment, is bankrupt.

What happened?

Zack met with Jesus. They had lunch together. Zack is so taken by Jesus that everything he was going for before doesn't seem to matter any more, compared to what Jesus is talking about.

Now we must not underestimate how important money and possessions are to Zack. He has stolen from loads of people. Loads of people know he has stolen from them. When people know someone is stealing from them, they don't tend to send that person Christmas cards. Zack is not well-liked.

We all like to be liked. Some people say they don't care whether people like them or not, but I don't believe them.

I have a reputation for being outspoken. I go around saying that I don't care what people think about me: if I am speaking the truth then I just have to take the consequences. I doubt Elijah had many friends, but he seemed to do the business for God, so why should I be any different?

Then one day I heard that, when asked, 'Where is Grant these days?', someone said, 'Oh, he's gone off to train to become a fascist dictator.'

Well, of course, that didn't affect me at all – much!

We all, whether we are prepared to admit it or not, care to some extent about what others think of us. The reason I am prepared to stick my neck out and say the things I do is because I believe, deep down, that what I'm saying is right. However, I suffer the consequences.

Zack knows he is not liked, but he thieved because having the stretched donkey and the balcony and the good living standard were more important to him than friends. Now that makes those things pretty important. But Zack speaks to Jesus for a couple of hours and gives it all away. Suddenly, in a moment, or a couple of hours, he realises there is something in life which means so much more than a stretched donkey.

And Jesus says, 'He just got saved.'

Did Jesus tell Zack that the only way he could be saved was to do the above? I don't know, but I doubt he did.

I guess that it's possible Jesus did say, 'Go out there and make a ridiculous statement and trust me.' But I doubt he did.

I think Zack was so excited that he just went over the top.

Let's be clear about what Zack did not do.

He did *not* come out on the balcony and say, 'I have been a thief and a bounder for years and years, but I have just realised how wrong I have been. I have repented of my sin and asked Jesus to come into my heart.'

What he did was to come out on his balcony and say, 'Jesus is more important than anything else in my life.'

And Jesus says, 'He just got saved.'

So, what does it mean to be a Christian?

3 WHAT'S MINE?

If money can't buy you happiness,
you'll just have to rent it.

I have a wife, Sue. She's great. I love her, she loves me, and she's mine.

That was straightforward enough.

I have three children, Vicky, Joseph and Samuel. I knew Sue (in the biblical sense of the word), because I lay with her and nine months later Sue was with child. After that, I lay with her two more times and two more nine-months-later Sue was with two more childs. These three children are mine. If there were any doubt about who the father was, you only have to spend some time with them to realise there is something of me in them all.

Some people say, 'Don't they look like their father?'

Others say, 'Don't they look like their mother?'

Either I look very much like Sue, or the people making those statements are basically looking at my features, or Sue's, and picking them out in the children. Alternatively, it could just be that the statement-makers are thinking, *Well, these two dorks are their parents, so it must be relatively safe to say that their children look like them.*

Are there any other features to indicate that the children are mine?

Vicky is very determined and always wants her own way. I think I can tell where she gets that from!

Samuel is a bit of a showman and never misses the

chance to make people laugh, although he fails on a regular basis. There's little doubt where he gets that from!

And Joseph?

One day, while sitting at the breakfast table, with cereal boxes all around, Joseph asked me, 'What is that word written on the cereal box?'

It was at the time when he was learning to spell and put words together, so Joe and I had this conversation.

Daddy:	What is the first letter?
Joe:	A.
Daddy:	What is the second letter?
Joe:	L.
Daddy:	What is the third letter?
Joe:	P.
Daddy:	What is the fourth letter?
Joe:	E.
	(Who's guessed it?)
Daddy:	What is the fifth letter?
Joe:	N?
Daddy:	And what does that spell then, Joe?
Joe:	Nod...

Now I can remember doing exactly that with my mother. The situation was different, but the outcome was the same. She, my mother, would stand there doing the ironing while she guided me through my spelling – with the consequence that my mother became very irate and frustrated with her son who was totally useless at spelling. Picture the scene: my mother standing at the ironing board, getting very red in the face, flailing this iron around – a frightening prospect, but it still didn't make my spelling any better.

So I guess I can see where Joe gets it from.

Therefore my children are mine...

I have a mother – she's mine, or I might be hers... Whatever, there is a 'mine' in there somewhere.

Jesus died for me. That's not mine, but it is *for* me.

I have one sister, three brothers-in-law, two sisters-in-law, three nieces and two nephews. I'm not sure that these are really mine, but they are certainly my family.

I have a few GCSEs – actually I lie, I have a few O levels, but I didn't want to give my age away. I have a few A levels and a few more qualifications. They all have my name on them and they are mine.

I have an ability to communicate – that's mine.

I have a few friends – they are mine.

I live in a house; you may be surprised to know that I own this – it's mine.

I drive a car – that's mine.

Then there's my sundry box in which there is a watch, blow-up dinghy, wedding photo, some letters from Sue, puncture-repair kit, highlighter pen, computer, spare inner tube, game of Pass the Pigs, Nelson Mandela's biography, Bible, Parker pen, *Space Jam* CD, squash racket, hole-punch and staple-remover.

They're all mine!

Now you have an almost comprehensive list of what is mine. Oh, and I did have a dog once, but that turned out to be an unfortunate experience and is best kept on a 'need to know' basis.

Back to my weakness for asking questions... Let's just have a quick look at how 'mine' these things are.

Sue, my wife, is mine, and I have instilled in her that the Bible says the commitment we have made is 'until death us do part'. But she may choose not to abide by the Bible and think she knows better and one day never come home again. I bet she would probably take the children too, because she knows she could bring them up better than me. So is Sue really mine? Or is this just a temporary arrangement while things are working, and one day it could all be gone?

I have three brilliant children and, whether they leave home at sixteen or sponge off us till the day I die, they are mine even if I never see them. I will always be their dad; they will always be my children.

But why do I have children? The miracle of birth only happened because God gave me fertile sperm with which to fertilise Sue's egg. I am not convinced I can take much credit for that. Only God can take the credit for every new creation. Parents' responsibility is simply then to bring that child up for God.

Many parents believe they have a right to their children until such time as there is no more breath in their bodies. I remember talking once to a mother of an eighteen-year-old girl who was dating a guy (the teenage daughter, not the mother). It was approaching Christmas and the teenage daughter was going to be spending Christmas with the guy's family. I said to the mother that I guessed she must find this hard. She replied something like this: 'God gave Kate to us, and it was our responsibility to do everything we could to give her a loving upbringing and to show her how much God loves her. Now she has got to the age where she doesn't need any more bringing-up, so my job is done. If Kate wants to spend time with me, that's a bonus, but it's not my right. Kate is God's, not mine. I just had the privilege of bringing her up for a while.'

Put like that, are my children mine?

What about my mother? Well, she is only mine for the same reason as the above, and the fact that God has given her life. My father died when I was ten and I think it's only because God still gives my mother life that she hasn't gone the same way as my father. So she is mine, but only because God has chosen it that way.

Jesus is mine. Now there's a subject...

In-laws: please see above.

Qualifications are mine

At last we have got to something that must be mine. I am the one who went through all that hard work. I did the course work. I revised. I studied. I kept going when others gave up. My name is on the certificate. These qualifications are mine, despite what happened at my eleven plus...

My parents were very keen for me to pass the eleven plus and I can remember sitting the exams. Come the day, I was probably the most prepared person in the room. One of the first questions we had was this: 'Which is heavier – a pound of lead or a pound of feathers?'

Now I knew this was a trick question because it was obvious that lead is heavier than feathers. But I also knew that we would never be asked such a simple question. So, seeing through the trickery of the examiner and knowing that many would fall at this hurdle, I wrote down, 'A pound of feathers.' I didn't know why, but I was confident I had caught them out. I can only imagine that the other trick questions were more subtle than this one, as I ended up failing!

But where did I get my brain from, to be able to have the concentration to achieve the other qualifications I have achieved? If God had given me a cabbage instead of a brain, no amount of study or effort or revision would have got me a driving licence, let alone certificates in anything.

So, are my qualifications mine, or are they simply what God has allowed me to have?

I have an ability to communicate. I go to schools; they invite me back. I go to universities; they invite me back. I go to churches; a few of them invite me back (but some don't like the message and ask me to leave early). I write books; you buy them.

The reason I can communicate is because I have been on public-speaking courses. My conclusion is that I am able to communicate because of an ability I have developed.

Somebody asked me once what I thought of spiritual gifts, and could it possibly be that this communication business is a gift from God?

Some people over-spiritualise everything!

Friends must be mine (although some would argue that people only put up with me because I am married to such a lovely wife).

The house is mine, or the bank's, depending on how you look at it. Regardless of who has the deeds, it is certainly me who pays for it every month.

However, if I didn't have the brain God gave me, I wouldn't have the job my qualifications allow me to have. And I wouldn't be able to pay the mortgage.

If I had been born in a land with an unstable and corrupt government and had no chance to study, I wouldn't have the qualifications, the job, the mortgage or the house.

The car is mine.

Actually, it's a company car. If I wasn't born in a stable country...

My sundry box is mine?

Something must be!

As you begin to break it all down, is there anything you can really call mine (or yours, depending on your viewpoint).

Recently, I was away with about 150 other people, and we had what we found out afterwards was a Rich/Poor Meal.

What happened was this – we all walked into the dining room, and the tables were laid as normal with the food already on them. The difference was that the dishes with the food in were all covered up, so nobody had any idea what they were getting. When the lids were removed, it was revealed that the right-hand side of the room had a good meal and the left-hand side of the room had some bread and very weak-looking soup.

At first the poor side complained, but they started on their bread and soup while the rich side began dishing out meat, vegetables and potatoes.

After a while, some of the poor tables began sending representatives over to the rich tables to ask if they could spare any food. And what tended to happen was that the rich tables would finish serving their people before giving the rep from the poor table the little that was left over after everyone on the rich table had been supplied with their requirement. Consequently, all the rich side of the room fed very well, thank you, and the poor side shared the equivalent of one portion between about ten people.

As the meal went on, people on the poor tables – with whom you had been talking and working all weekend – started to become mildly abusive. A few on the rich tables actually had seconds. Interestingly enough, one of the leaders roaming around the tables afterwards commented that those on the poor tables talked about nothing else other than the fact they were hungry and how much the rich side had, while the rich tables talked about anything and everything.

In this simple illustration, staged at a Tearfund event where people were sympathetic to the Tearfund cause, the attitude prevailed that 'this food was dished up on the table I am sitting on and therefore it is mine'. The rich half hadn't paid any more for that meal and the poor half hadn't paid any less. However, there was still the strong feeling that 'possession is nine-tenths of the law and you lot just made a bad choice'.

You and I both know that nobody could actually say, 'This is mine', but reality revealed that we tend to think differently. At this Tearfund event we couldn't even get 150 people in the same room to share fairly among themselves, let alone share with others on the opposite side of the world. The sad part of the story is, all those present were there to discuss helping the poor, and were about to go out and work with the poor for the next five or six weeks of their lives. However, in the space of about thirty minutes, perhaps their true colours were revealed.

As you have guessed by now, I am married.

I think it's great.

I think my wife is great.

I think my children are great.

I think my home is great.

I think cheese is grate.

I was, however, a confirmed bachelor boy. Several experiences had put me off marriage, not least the fact that I wasn't convinced I knew anyone who was happily married. It seemed to me that people had great fun going out; then they became a little more isolated and serious when they got engaged, and downright miserable when they got married.

I was quite content to stay single – until I met Sue. She threw a spanner in the works. There was something different about her and, after some time, I asked her to marry me. After that hurdle was crossed, the trouble and the questions began.

What if I get fed up?

What if Sue falls out of love with me?

What if I want to go to Russia and Sue doesn't?

What if Sue turns into a raving *Star Trek* fan?

I became convinced that I couldn't pull off my side of the deal and I wasn't going to be fair to Sue. So Sue got me all these books on marriage. I must have read about five of them. To save you the trouble of spending all that money on books, I will sum them up here.

Go into marriage expecting nothing and prepared to give everything.

I thought you went into marriage with the view, 'What's mine is mine and what's yours is mine'. However, the books were saying something a little different. In effect, they were saying that *nothing* is mine.

I could see this working if *Sue* adopted the ideal marriage stance, but I wasn't convinced that *I* could.

After some debate in my head and talking it through with friends, I came to the conclusion that all the evidence pointed towards the model promoted in the books working. (Mind you, I couldn't help wondering if the books had been written by people who were hoping their partners would read them and subsequently adopt the model!) My experience has proved the rule, which has been further proved since the arrival of sprogs. I have been married fourteen years and I still get excited about seeing Sue after I have been away on a visit. Not that I don't get excited about seeing her when I'm not on a visit, but especially when I've been away. It doesn't matter whether I go away for a weekend or a month – the last little bit is the worst, because all I want to do is get home and see Sue and the children.

Nothing is mine – not money, not clothes, not time, not even the burnt crispy bits left behind after the roast has been dished up. Absolutely nothing.

The conclusion I have come to (although using illustrations usually breaks down somewhere) is that in marriage it has to be a conscious decision that nothing is your own. Actually, this is quite an easy decision to make when you realise that, in marriage or otherwise, nothing is your own anyway.

And if nothing is my own, what right do I have to cling to so much of what has come my way?

Just today I was talking to someone I work with, who said something like, 'My wife and I think that we have had such good lives, if we don't give something back we might suffer the consequences.'

> What right have I got to eat three square meals a day when children are starving to death?
>
> What right have I got to a four-bedroom house when 14 million people are refugees?
>
> What right have I got to good health when 40,000 children die every day of preventable diseases?
>
> What right have I got to a power shower when millions don't have clean water to drink?
>
> What right have I got to a pension when one billion people live on less than a dollar per day?
>
> What right have I got to a turbo-charged, fuel-injected, air-conditioned, leather-upholstered power...?

Some of you may be thinking, *How far is he going to go?*

You tell me.

You tell me the answers when we face the Creator one day, when we're sitting in the waiting room to our eternal destiny next to a starved refugee who has spent her life waiting to die.

What will we say when God asks us, 'So what did *you* do with what I gave you?'

'Well ... I reckoned it was mine'?

4 WHAT ABOUT JESUS?

Life started off simple.
Then, to make life easier,
man made machines.
Then machines became so complicated,
they gave man a headache.

One day, about five minutes after breakfast, my son Joseph said to Sue, 'I'm hungry.'

Sue's response was, 'Well, that's tough. You should have eaten all your breakfast, then perhaps you wouldn't be.'

My daughter, Vicky, never wanting to miss the opportunity to get one-up on her brother and knowing that on this particular day she had eaten all her breakfast, then said, 'I'm hungry.'

Sue's response to Vicky was, 'You can't possibly be, you've just eaten all your breakfast.'

Parents always seem to have an answer to keep control of their children (when they are young). However, the answers aren't so readily available as the questions get harder.

Gallons of ink have been consumed in explaining the positioning of commas, full stops and 'therefores' in the Bible. The reason for this is so that the average pew-warmer has some sort of guide to life.

There once was a Bible college lecturer whose specialist subject was Ephesians.

One day per week was his study day. During this day he studied Ephesians.

One term every three years was a sabbatical term. During this term he studied Ephesians.

One year in every nine years was a sabbatical year. During this year he studied Ephesians.

He had worked at the college for over twenty years.

One day a friend of mine went into his office and asked this lecturer what he considered was the overall meaning of the book of Ephesians.

His answer? 'I'm really not sure.'

Really not sure!

What do you mean, *'Really not sure'*?

You're the expert. You're the one whose studied it for years. You could probably write it better yourself. And you're *really not sure?*

If you asked *me* what was the overall meaning of any bit of the Bible, I've got an answer. So what on earth does this guy mean by saying, 'Really not sure'?

He knows far more than any of us, but his response is, 'Really not sure'.

I have an answer for any Bible bit you like. But lecturer matey? On his specialist subject? And the answer is, 'Really not sure'?

Who's got it right?

I've interpreted the Bible at a very simplistic level into my culture and lifestyle so that I can either justify my way of life or claim to have understanding. But the more our lecturer friend looks at Ephesians, he concludes, 'Really not sure.'

The reality is, I can't really be that sure either. The Bible is a very complex book. A superficial understanding of it may lead to our ignoring the bits that don't fit our philosophy or using the bits that do fit to further our own cause. Some people spend so much time going to Bible studies and listening to sermons in their attempts to develop an understanding of God, when perhaps all they really need to do is to take a long, hard look at Jesus, who he was and what he did. After all, the Bible tells us about God, and Jesus was God: can't we bypass the words and look at the real person?

You see, I can use Bible verses to back up anything! Well, most things...

Genesis 16:1–4: It's fine to have affairs.

Deuteronomy 24:1–4: Divorce is fine.

1 Samuel 18:7: Murder is fine.

Matthew 19:21: The best Christian gives everything to the poor.

Matthew 26:11: You always have poor people, so there's nothing you can do about it.

Luke 16:9: If you get rich, you will get saved.

John 16:24: Ask for anything and you can have it.

Romans 8:28: Don't worry, it will all come good eventually.

2 Corinthians 12:7–9: God doesn't heal.

This may be a little simplistic, but one only has to have a concordance and a few more references and we'd be on our way to the above becoming true.

I wonder if instead we should devote more time simply trying to understand how Jesus lived. If ever we have been sent a role model, he must be it.

Let's look at Jesus

We don't read that Jesus owned anything. No home, no car, no holiday villa, unless of course you count heaven as being a holiday villa. No pension, no insurance, no

CDs, no designer labels, no music centre. Absolutely nothing. I assume that he did own some things, but they obviously weren't considered significant enough to mention.

When Jesus employed disciples, there was no mention of terms and conditions. No salary, no hours, no notice period, no perks.

Possibly this helps us to understand Peter and John when they were on their way to the temple and a cripple asked them for money and they said, 'We have no money. But we do know Jesus, so walk' (Acts 3:1–10).

The impression we get is that Jesus lived a simple life. We also seem to get the impression that he encouraged those close to him to do the same. He taught that we should trust God for our basic needs, and the life he lived demonstrates how we can do that.

If the only significant event in Jesus' life was his death and resurrection, then all he would have done is die and resurrect. But he didn't. He came and lived thirty-three years, thirty of which we know almost nothing about, and three of which are considered so important four guys wrote about them and their accounts are included in the Bible.

His life leading up to the cross *is* significant because it provides us with a practical guide to living. I am convinced that to understand how we are meant to live today, we need to understand the logic behind how Jesus lived then.

If a simple lifestyle was good enough for Jesus, where do we fit in? And why do we spend years trying to interpret complex verses, when the answers Jesus gives us are probably more straightforward than we think?

Admittedly, there are a few difficulties. Jesus never got married, he died on a cross, he was conceived by the Holy Spirit and he talked freely to Samaritans.

Consequently, if all the answers are found in Jesus, nobody gets married, we must die for our faith, we have no physical father and we have to talk to today's equivalent to the Samaritans, the Basildonians.

So there is weakness in my argument. But I think we can understand *in general* the point that is being made.

Possibly a bigger problem than our failure to let Jesus be our role model is this: if we look in our churches, there are very few lifestyle role models who come anywhere near Jesus.

The role models we have tell us that church is important and status quo rules OK.

How many people do you know personally who are living on the edge for Jesus or come anywhere near the example he set? How many people can you name in your church who have any sort of long-term ambition for God? How many people in your church don't give a monkey's armpit what house they live in or what car they drive or what clothes they wear?

Despite what the Bible says about modelling ourselves on Jesus, we look instead at the church and think, *I'm no worse than anyone else*, because the role models are so pathetic.

I once did a survey amongst a group of kids whose parents were churchgoers. I asked them to write down three ambitions or goals they had for the next twenty years. All of them, without exception, said careers, marriage and financial security. Why? Because their parents and their parents' mates say one thing but live something else. Not one of those in the survey had any goal for God.

Maybe I got them on a bad day or maybe they lied. Or maybe they knew the answers I was looking for and decided to stuff me right up. But I don't think so.

I recently went with a group of students to Kenya.

When they came home, they were all fired up and wanted to do loads of things to make a difference. Within one week of our return, I had spoken to two of those students, and both of them said that their parents, who were good churchgoers, had sat on all their ideas and squeezed out their enthusiasm.

Why?

Because they looked at all the reasons why those ideas wouldn't work instead of wondering whether God might actually just want to accomplish something through their offspring's enthusiasm. Oh yes, I'm sure it was the wisdom of experience that led them to their oppression, but wasn't there another possibility? That the ideas might just work?

Thus it is from an early age our elders teach us how to approach every issue with dead-steady logic instead of Holy Spirit power.

I know there are some exceptions to the above, but in general these are the role models we have. They are nice people, I don't doubt, but role models for Christianity they are not.

The consequence is, we are left thinking that those who go all out for God are just the superheroes like Jackie Pullinger and Steve Chalke and Matt Redman. We could never hope to be like them, so let's be humdrum.

Tony Campolo is a Christian American lecturer in sociology renowned for his work with the poor. He has said something like this: 'You cannot call yourself a Christian and own a BMW.'

He says that many people have questioned him on this and – yes – he really did mean it.

Why? Because a BMW is a status symbol, and he can't imagine Jesus driving a status symbol while children died.

He actually says more than that, but if you want to know what this is, he's written about it in *20 Hot Potatoes Christians are Afraid to Touch* (Word, 1988).

I once told this story at a presentation I was doing for Tearfund. Somebody came up to me at the end and said, 'I couldn't help thinking while you were talking that I was glad I didn't own a BMW.'

After talking with me, he walked out of the building and got into his Jag...

When it was reported that Guy Snowden attempted to bribe Richard Branson over the bidding for the lottery, a report on News at Ten suggested that the following conversation took place:

GS: Everybody has his or her price.

RB: I can only eat one breakfast, one lunch and one dinner a day, and I'm already doing that.

Admittedly, Richard Branson's idea of basic needs for living may be slightly different from mine, but the concept is certainly there.

Jesus described who our neighbours are and who our brothers and sisters are. Would you let your brother go hungry while you ate caviar and cream?

No.

Then Jesus' words cannot be conveniently ignored.

Whether you like it or not, you are a role model now and you are going to be the role model of the future. You can't avoid this, no matter what you do.

What are you going to pass on?

Something of the life of Jesus?

Or something of Western-status-quo-mediocrity-church-culture?

Try saying that with bubble gum in your mouth.

5 WHAT SHOULD I GIVE?

Money is the root of evil –
and we all need roots.

We have a friend who, in the notes at the back of his personal organiser, has a diagram of his garden, marking the location of the hole for their whirligig washing-line.

Intrigued at this detail, I asked why.

His response? So that when it snows, they would still be able to hang out their washing.

Good point, although I must confess I don't know many people who hang their washing out in the snow. Normally, when snow is on the ground, the temperature is less than zero degrees centigrade. The reason for hanging washing out is because it is wet. Water tends to freeze at zero degrees centigrade. Consequently, not many people hang out their washing. Call me an old traditionalist, but I'm not convinced.

Is giving a precise science?

Whenever Christians think of giving, many automatically think of tithing (ie giving ten per cent of what we earn). If we do tithe, we tend to think that we have this giving business sussed. If we don't tithe, we have several good reasons why we don't, or we feel bad.

Current research shows that the bulk of church giving comes from the older members of our community. The younger people have mortgages. That's not really a problem though, because there will always be older people to balance out the giving of the younger element.

The only trouble is, those older members who are the big givers now were the big givers when they were young too. This, therefore, indicates a disappointing trend. Though tithing is seen as biblical in theory, the reality is that it isn't happening in the young community.

There's an old song that goes:

All to Jesus I surrender,
all to Him I freely give...

Tony Campolo, who featured in the last chapter, began a talk once by singing that song. Only he changed the words to:

Ten per cent to Jesus I surrender,
Ten per cent I freely give...

Tithing is mentioned ten times in the Old Testament and four times in the New. So at least it's a diminishing trend...

In summary. We read that Abraham tithed (Gen 14:20). There is one directive in Leviticus that ten per cent of the land belongs to God (Lev 27:30). By Numbers, Deuteronomy and Chronicles, there are four instructions that tithes be given to the Levites (ie Old Testament vicar types), of which ten per cent of the ten per cent should be given to God (Num 18:21; Deut 14:28–29; 26:12; 2 Chron 31:4–5; Neh 10:38). There are two further records of tithing happening (Neh 12:44; 13:12), and one endorsement by Amos (4:4). Malachi warns that if you don't tithe, you are stealing (Mal 3:8–10).

In the New Testament, there are three references to the pompous Pharisees (Matt 23:23; Luke 11:42; 18:11–12).

So what?

Is it biblical to tithe?

It is definitely mentioned in the Bible, but does it apply to today?

It would appear that in the Old Testament the majority of the tithe went to pay the Levites rather than to help out the poor. But then there were the rules of Jubilee which were there to protect the poor. We will look at these later.

So if, in the Old Testament, tithing was to pay the clergy, and this still applies today, who helps the poor? Perhaps we are meant to pay the tithe to support the minister and then give again for the poor?

I suppose there is one further aspect we should consider, which is that today we are taxed by the government. I don't think this happened in the Old Testament to the same extent, although we know that little Zack did his best to promote the idea later on. Is it not therefore the responsibility of the taxman to use the tax money to help the poor? After all, we pay enough in tax. They say it's 23 per cent, but that's just propaganda. Look.

> You earn £1.00 and you get taxed at 23 per cent. So tax is 23p; you keep 77p.
>
> You spend the 77p that's left on your helper-lady washing your windows. She gets taxed at 23 per cent. So tax is 18p; window-washer keeps 59p.
>
> Window-washer has hairdresser come to her home and spends 59p on a perm. Perm man gets taxed at 23 per cent. So tax is 14p; perm man has 45p.
>
> Perm man spends 45p on a gardener. Gardener gets taxed at 23 per cent. Tax is 10p; gardener has 35p.
>
> Gardener spends 35p on a shoeshine. Shoeshine gets

taxed at 23 per cent. Tax is 8p; shoeshine gets 27p.

Shoeshine spends 27p on a massage. Masseur gets taxed at 23 per cent. Tax is 6p; masseur gets 21p.

Masseur spends 21p on a man to clean the carpets. Carpet-cleaner gets taxed at 23 per cent. Tax is 5p; carpet-cleaner gets 16p.

Carpet-cleaner spends 16p on a flower for his girlfriend. Flower-lady gets taxed at 23 per cent. Tax is 4p; flower-lady gets 12p.

Flower-lady spends 12p as a tip to the coffee-shop waiter. Waiter, who declares tips, gets taxed at 23 per cent. Tax is 3p; waiter gets paid 9p.

Waiter spends 9p on a hand wheel-wash (couldn't afford the whole car). Wheel-washer gets taxed at 23 per cent. Tax is 2p; wheel-washer gets 7p.

While on holiday in Kenya, wheel-washer gives 7p to a bag lady. Kenyan bag lady is taxed at about 40 per cent...

It's probably best to stop there!

But the point is, of the original pound, 93p ended up in British tax. Surely they can do something about the poor?

The answer to that question is, 'They do.'

But still 40,000 children die every night from preventable diseases.

So who pays?

Forget tithing!

Tithing is either Old Testament history or pay the clergy: it has nothing to do with the poor. The taxman isn't doing enough in the UK, let alone elsewhere. So what do we do?

I don't have a problem with people earning big money. It's what happens to the money that matters.

Some time ago the following situation occurred in my life. I was getting a lift in a car whose driver made this statement: 'I believe God has given me the gift to make money.'

Interesting, I thought, *I don't remember Paul saying, 'The third spiritual gift is making loads of dosh.'*

But then, if you read Paul carefully, taking his comments on spiritual gifts as your specialist subject on *Mastermind*, what would your answer be if old Magness Magnissan asked, 'What is the third spiritual gift?'

The answer would have to be 'Pass.'

Nowhere in the Bible is there a finite list of spiritual gifts. Call me an old traditionalist, but that would suggest to me that there isn't one.

'Why no list?' I hear you ask.

Well, I don't know, but it could be because God dishes out spiritual gifts as and when the need arises or when they are specific to different cultures or situations, and therefore Paul didn't know what would be needed and when it would be needed.

In the car, as this whole thought process whizzed through my head, I thought, *Cool. Because the gift of making money is needed today, this guy has been given that gift.*

However, having worked my way through the above, I still wasn't exactly sure what he meant by his statement. I therefore asked him to explain. The conversation went something like this:

Billy: I started out life in a low-paid job and, all things being equal, this is what I would have done until the day I died.

Me: Are all things not equal then?

Billy: What I mean is, I could never have anticipated earning the money I do today, given the way I started out. I really believe that it is God who has helped me do what I do. As a result, I tithe my money. Therefore, because I earn so much, the amount of the tithe is much bigger than it ever has been before. I believe that it is God who has gifted me to make money.

I knew that Billy lived in a substantial home and had approximately six cars on his drive (although it was difficult to keep count because they kept moving about).

I was also aware that we were a long way from home and it was a cold night and I was in Billy's car. However, I had another question. Should I leave it until we were nearer home?

Stupidity being the better part of discretion, I launched into my response which went something like this:

Me: Rubbish!

This blurted out of my mouth for some reason I can't really explain, but blurted out it did. And now it kind of sat on the dashboard with us both looking at it, and I knew that it was still my turn to speak. So I continued:

Me: If I have the gift of prophecy, what do I do with it? Do I use ninety per cent of it to make me loads of money as a lecturer and give ten per cent of it to the church?

No. It is a gift from God and I use it to build God's kingdom.

I had started now, so I had to finish.

Me: If I have the gift of healing, what do I do with it? Do I use ninety per cent to make me loads

> of money as a surgeon and give ten per cent of it to the church?
>
> No. It is a gift from God and I use it to build God's kingdom.
>
> You have just said that you have the gift of making money. What have you done with it?
>
> Used ninety per cent of it to build *your* kingdom and given ten per cent to God.

The walk home wasn't so bad. Once you have negotiated a couple of hours in subzero temperatures without a coat on, one mile just fades into another and you lose count eventually. They say the frostbite damage will improve eventually, although I think 'eventually' might mean 'in heaven'. But hey, in the scope of eternity that's not far off now.

Some of you may remember in 1998 there was a World Cup that took place in France. Hand in hand with any major football event is football hooliganism. The World Cup was no exception. On TV we were told that at this World Cup, however, the English police and French police were working together. They were picking out the so-called ringleaders and sending them home before they even got a chance to cause trouble.

On the news one night, a bunch of these fans were pictured returning to England's shores. A Very Intellectual Journalist had her camera-person shoot her going up to a fan, Possible Hooligan, and having this conversation:

VIJ: You have just been sent home from France.

PH: *(Innocent until proven guilty)* Oh, have I?

VIJ: Did you go to cause trouble?

PH: Who me? Don't even know what trouble is!

Possible Hooligan was hardly going to say, 'Trouble? Of course I went to cause trouble! Those French deserved to be kicked, and there was nobody else there to do it so I just felt I had to!' No more than we are going to admit that we have turned our back on the role model Jesus has given us.

I have another friend (it's best to have a few, in case you upset one of them). This friend's earning capacity is approximately £2,000 per day. Yes, that's right – per day. Not per week or per month. She lives in a three-bedroom terraced house and drives an Escort. She takes her holidays in Bognor Regis and she has no pension.

I guess you are wondering what she does spend her money on. She uses it to fund her God-ambition and what she believes she can do for God.

Here is a person who recognises that it is God who has given her the money she has and therefore the money belongs to God.

A few years ago I believe God challenged Sue and myself about the need to go to Bible college. We had children and obviously the big issue was how would we survive financially. We prayed that if this was God's burden, the church would come to us and say, 'We believe you should go to Bible college. Here is £20,000. Off you go, and see you in three years.' Well, I believe in miracles. Don't you?

But, as you have probably guessed, this never happened.

One day I felt that God had given me a vision that if I went freelance in my work, I could probably earn twice what I was currently earning and fund Bible college that way. So this is what I did.

Within six months I was earning something like five times what I had been earning before. The business had its own bank account, and we drew off the business what I had previously earned because we considered that, as God had given us this idea, the rest of the money must be his.

If you believe God has filled you with the Holy Spirit and given you the brains and the chance in life to do what you are doing; if you believe that he has a purpose for your life which goes beyond singing hymns or choruses and becoming a deacon; if you believe that your life can make a difference and God leads you into being successful in business; then I believe God wants to see something more from your life than a tithe.

God wants to see business that is run with a Christian ethos. Not the typical business where you get away with paying everybody the least you can so that you can make more. Not the typical business where you push your employees so hard, they end up in broken marriages and depression.

God wants to see Christian businesses that people look at and say, 'There's something radically different going on here.' God wants to see successful business Christians who measure success not by the houses they live in and the cars they drive, but by the impact Jesus is making in every life that their business touches.

Christians are not standing out. Christians are no different. You show me one Christian executive who drives a Ford Fiesta and I'll show you a rarity.

If you are serious about making a difference, then why not use the skills you learned at university to revolutionise the workplace into one where people *want* to be because the ethos of the business is more concerned with people than with making mone?. You do that and you will evangelise far more people than you will ever do by preaching.

John Laing started his own construction company in the 1930s. He was very successful. Let me tell you some of the things he did.

His company formed a benevolent fund for loyal workers.

His company pioneered the practice of giving their operatives paid holidays.

When Laing visited his construction sites, he had a reputation for speaking to anybody, from the man with the shovel to the largest client.

Laing was respected for his insight into construction methods.

Laing was a millionaire. In the biography of his life, there is a story of how one of his friends bought him a Rolls Royce, but he turned it down because he was quite happy with his Rover.

He died with £371 to his name because he had given the rest away.

Today the Laing Trust is still in existence, operated by trustees who are still investing and making grants for purposes they believe Laing would have supported.*

Laing was a man empowered by God. When he touched people's lives, they saw something of Jesus.

Note

* From the biography of Sir John W Laing CBE, *Laing*.

6 GIVE THEM THE GOSPEL

When I were a wee lad, I used to go to the Gospel Hall. You don't tend to see many of those these days in England, but if you go to Scotland or Ireland there are a few more. At the Gospel Hall they always had a gospel service in the evening where the gospel had to be preached.

I also remember going to see my grandmother in Dumfries in Scotland. She went to a Gospel Hall and, in the summer, they would have the gospel service 'down on the sands' – a term I never really understood because 'The Sands' was a pavement between the bus depot and the river. I didn't let that worry me though, because while the gospel service was going on you could watch the salmon jumping up the river – much more fun than playing word-games with the text at the front of the church.

There was one church I went to for years which had John 3:16 as their text, written up on a big board just above the lectern. I spent many a happy hour trying to make up all sorts of phrases just using the words from John 3:16, such as:

Perish the world for eternal beliefs.

And…

Whoever believes in life will love the world.

You can see that the gospel had quite an impact on my life from an early age. But what do all these people mean by 'gospel'? David Evans of Tearfund made this statement at an orientation course I went to:

Christianity is not a philosophy, because it doesn't stack up. It is a lifestyle.

Now I loved that statement. I wasn't convinced at the time it was right, but I wanted to be able to prove that it was.

The reason I thought it was so good is this: if it can be proved that Christianity is not a philosophy, yet if a person's life does not change as a result of meeting Jesus, then what is Christianity?

Absolutely nothing.

Now *that* is worth thinking about.

The next time I went out preaching I decided to talk about this statement and prove it, with audience participation. When I had finished speaking, I asked the gathered congregation for a response.

I told them that I knew there were many who disagreed with me. I also knew they would go home and dismiss me over their Sunday roast. But I didn't like people talking behind my back, so I wanted to know what they thought now. Plus, if they didn't point out where I was wrong, I would believe I was right and go to the next church and preach the same. So speak to me.

As you can imagine, there was silence for some time. Then one man said something which was more or less irrelevant. Then – just like a spot on your face which you have been squeezing gently – splat! Out it came.

'Do you believe you have preached the gospel today?' asked one pew-warmer.

'Now that is an excellent question,' I retorted. 'Absolutely brilliant. Do I believe I have preached the gospel?

'Before I can answer that question,' I said, 'can you tell me what the gospel is?'

The questioner was obviously far too wise for me and ready for such a question. He shot back immediately: 'No. You're the preacher. You should be telling *us*.'

So, boxed into a corner with no way out, my only response was to come out with guns blazing.

'I work part-time for Tearfund which is regarded by traditionalists as a Social Action Organisation. I also work for Viz-A-Viz which is regarded by traditionalists as an Organisation That Spreads The Gospel. How do I come to terms with pulling these two extremes together, when often I am standing on a stage with a microphone in my hand representing both at the same time?

'Well, I'll tell you.

'There is *no* distinction between social action and gospel. When Jesus came to earth, he died on a cross and came back to life again three days later. As a result, everybody has the chance to know God for ever. This is a fundamental step in having a relationship with Jesus. But his death was only *one part* of his life. He also lived a life. We read that he was baptised. We read that he was full of the Holy Spirit. We read that he talked to prostitutes, healed the sick, cared for the hungry, ate with bad guys, cared for the poor, lived simply, preached, loved children... 'Jesus *is* the gospel.

'You may have noticed that we read all this stuff in 'the Gospels'. The gospel is huge, far bigger than Jesus dying on a cross, crucial as that may be.'

I paused for breath at this point and then went back to the questioner: 'Do you therefore consider that I have preached the gospel this morning?'

'In part, I suppose,' was his response.

The issue is that many people, when they talk about the gospel, really mean 'the story of the cross'. To them, unless the word 'cross' is mentioned the gospel has not been preached.

We have all heard the story of the birth of Jesus told in many different ways. It seems to me that every Christmas another piece is added to the story which makes it worse than the year before. This year I heard that Jesus didn't even get to the stable to be born, but was actually born on the streets. Next year we will probably find out that not only was he born in the streets, but Mary was sitting over a manhole at the time. Unfortunately, the manhole collapsed at the time of birth and the baby dropped twenty-five feet into the sewer below. And still 'no crying he makes'...

However bad it gets, we know Jesus wasn't born in a comfy hospital.

Why?

Why did Jesus have to suffer all that humiliation? If some inquisitive journalist dug around and found out that Tony Blair was actually the illegitimate child of unmarried parents and born in some road-side services toilet, I am sure we would get to hear about it.

Headline:

BLAIR BORN IN SCOTTISH SERVICE STATION EXPLAINS DESIRE FOR DEVOLUTION

Old Tony, I am sure, would not be exactly proud of such a situation, and I don't suppose it was any different for Jesus (although I'm not sure what Jesus would have thought about devolution).

The whole of Jesus' life *is* the gospel. It is *all* significant. It is all there for our understanding and as a model for life. If it wasn't, then Jesus wouldn't have done it and we wouldn't know.

I visited a slum once, in Nairobi, which was introduced to us as the worst slum in the world. I am not exactly sure who compiles these league tables of slums and what constitutes the status of being the worst. Certainly I have visited a few in my life and this one wasn't good. But then none of them were places I would particularly want to move to. Suffice to say, it was rough.

While there, I was chatting to the pastor who led a church that was actually right in the middle of the slum. There were something like 20,000 people living in the area. The pastor explained to me that when he first came to the slum, he couldn't have walked through it without a minder – and I would probably have needed an army of minders, as I am white and pathetic-looking. Now, however, he could walk freely whether day or night.

I was obviously intrigued to know why this was the case, so I asked, 'Why is this the case?'

He said, 'I believe that the church has brought a new atmosphere to the slum. People have seen that we care about them. We have fed their children. We have shown love. We have shared what we have. And we have helped with their education. As a consequence, parents have wanted to come to the church and to find out why we do what we do, what is our motivation. We tell them about Jesus. As a result many people want to become disciples and the atmosphere in the slum has changed. This doesn't mean that all the population has turned to God, but the influence of those who have has changed the attitude of those who, at the moment, don't think Jesus is for them.

'However,' the pastor continued, 'there is a downside.'

I was obviously intrigued to know why there was a downside, so I asked, 'Why is there a downside?'

He said, 'Many people, when they find out how much Jesus loves them, want to become disciples. As a consequence of becoming disciples, they realise that they are important to God and gain much higher self-worth. As a result of higher self-worth, it makes the families want to work harder for their children and for themselves, because of their increased self-esteem. Ultimately, they improve their lives and are able to move out of the slum. So we lose their influence in the community.'

My brain went into whizzing mode again as I considered what the pastor had just said. In simple terms, he was saying that by giving bread to children and helping in their education, parents met with Jesus. They realised their self-worth and had the incentive to work harder. This resulted in their being able to move out of the slum and thereby escape the poverty which had gripped them for years.

I had another question: 'If people are becoming disciples, gaining a new incentive to provide for their families and moving out of the slum – if *everybody* met with Jesus and became disciples – then would there, ultimately, be no slum?'

'Yes,' replied the pastor.

There, I believe, in the slum, is the gospel at work.

The difference between a church feeding the children and a relief organisation which has no concept of God feeding the children, is that the relief organisation only has part of the answer.

I have watched several videos on how Christians should bring up children. There was one video about helping your children deal with bullies at school. It went on to say that we should encourage our children, when approached by a potential bully, to stand in the playground and pray. Call me an old traditionalist, but I would tell my children to run like the clappers and when they get home, then we would pray. At least that way they'd be in a fit state to talk to God. I know prayer changes things, but there are practical ways of changing things. We need to open up our eyes to the full impact of the gospel. It is not about having 'quiet times' and going to church. In the slum, Christianity totally revolutionised lives.

I went to another slum which was not, according to the league tables of slums, the worst slum in the world. Definitely, conditions were not as bad. There, talking with a church member, I asked why he thought the church in Kenya was growing.

He said that he believed part of the reason was because parents were seeing that the church was prepared to educate their children, so the parents wanted to know why. When they discovered that the church simply cared for the lives of their children, they wanted to know what motivated the church to care. When they found out what motivated the church to care, they wanted to experience this same motivation. So they became disciples.

The Bible tells us to spread the gospel, but what is the gospel?

Jesus did not come just to preach; he came to show us how to live. The church has often been accused of going to Africa and other far-away places, and ramming British religion down people's throats. This accusation is probably true to some extent, if you think about it hard enough. But people the world over don't need to be told about religion; what they need is to see the lifestyle Jesus demonstrated. Then they can make up their own minds who God is.

Once when Samuel, my youngest son, was about two, I said that, as a special treat, he could stay up late to watch a video with his brother and sister. We all know that one of the most special treats you can give children is to stay up late. It's not only little children who want to do this: all ages of offspring find it a special treat to have permission to stay out later and later, until they just don't come home any more.

So I, being a big-hearted daddy who understood what all children wanted, let Samuel stay up late. After watching the video for ten minutes, Samuel looks up at me and says, 'Daddy, can I go to bed now?'

We can't just tell people what we think is the best way to be: we need to live the life Jesus is calling us to live, and then let them decide for themselves how they want to respond.

7 I'M STILL STANDING

If this were a musical pop-up storybook,
you would now be hearing the first line
of a song by Elton John.
But it's not. So you won't.

The Holy Spirit, I think, has become one of the most fraught subjects within the world of the church. And yet, debatably, the Holy Spirit plays the most significant part in our Christian lives. However, over the last few years, people's experiences have led to misunderstanding, confusion and fear. Possibly the questions that Christians are most often asking are, 'Do I have the Holy Spirit? and 'How will this affect me?'

Mind you, possibly nothing has changed much on the misunderstanding front. My parents' generation went around calling the Holy Spirit 'the Holy Ghost' which, given that they didn't believe in ghosts, caused a great deal of confusion. My generation changed 'Ghost' to 'Spirit' but were told to keep away from evil spirits and alcohol, so we were no better. Now this generation has to fall over, bawl their eyes out or roar like lions to be confirmed as 'Spirit-filled'.

A friend of ours was in church recently when the preacher made an appeal: 'If you want to receive the Holy Spirit afresh, then come down to the front.' (Funny how the Holy Spirit is always at the front.)

So Herbert (made-up name to protect the pressurised)

sits nailed to his chair, determined that this is not for him. He has been brought up with the understanding that when you become a disciple you receive the Holy Spirit and, although you may 'leak' a little, there is no need to go up the front to receive the Spirit again in front of three hundred other people. He has never needed to go forward before and he fails to see that there is any need to start now.

The challenge is given again, and Herbert starts to think: *Hang on! Although I don't doubt that I have the Holy Spirit in my life, I also know that my relationship with Jesus could be a lot better.*

Eventually, convinced that God is speaking to him, he decides the time has come, and up he goes.

Eleven other people have made the same response, and now all twelve of them are standing at the front of the church. The minister and a few others lay hands on each, one at a time. And this is what happens:

Candidate One: Place hands on upper body; prayer commences; candidate collapses like a pack of cards on the floor; prayer people move on to the next.

Candidate Two: Place hands on upper body; prayer commences; candidate collapses like a pack of cards on the floor; prayer people move on to the next.

Candidate Three: Place hands on upper body; prayer commences; candidate collapses like a pack of cards on the floor; prayer people move on to the next.

Candidate Four: Place hands on upper body; prayer commences; candidate collapses like a pack of cards on the floor; prayer people move on to the next.

Candidate Five: Place hands on upper body; prayer commences; candidate collapses like a pack of cards on the floor; prayer people move on to the next.

Candidate Six: Place hands on upper body; prayer commences; candidate collapses like a pack of cards on the floor; prayer people move on to the next.

Candidate Seven: Place hands on upper body; prayer commences; candidate collapses like a pack of cards on the floor; prayer people move on to the next.

Candidate Eight: Place hands on upper body; prayer commences; candidate collapses like a pack of cards on the floor; prayer people move on to the next.

Candidate Nine: Place hands on upper body; prayer commences; candidate collapses like a pack of cards on the floor; prayer people move on to the next.

Herbert: Place hands on upper body; prayer commences; Herbert stands still; prayer continues; Herbert stands still; prayer continues; Herbert stands still; Herbert obviously isn't going anywhere; prayer people move on to the next.

Candidate Eleven: Place hands on upper body; prayer commences; candidate collapses like a pack of cards on the floor; prayer people move on to the next.

Candidate Twelve: Place hands on upper body; prayer commences; candidate collapses like a pack of cards on the floor; prayer people move on.

Does Herbert still have the Holy Spirit as he thought he had when he first met Jesus, or has this experience superseded that part of his understanding?

Is Herbert resisting what God wants to do in his life?

Has Herbert got unconfessed sin isolating him from the Holy Spirit? (And now we are all having a guess at what that might be.)

Does Herbert have Hercules knees so that if an oak tree fell on him he would still be standing?

Does God treat all of us as individuals?

Have the other eleven received an additional anointing and Herbert hasn't?

Have the eleven buckled to expectations rather than the Spirit?

Herbert does not suffer from exuding confidence and high self-esteem at the best of times. How does he feel now?

There he is, all 6ft 6 of him. Looking to the left, nobody there. Looking to the right, nobody there. All around him, crumpled bodies. If this happened on a railway station platform, the eleven would be the oddballs and Herbert the normal one. It happens in a church, and the eleven are normal and Herbert is the oddball.

The above does not lend itself to a simple understanding of what Jesus left for us. Somehow I can't help feeling that we have made a pretty bad job of making understanding easy. I guess the problem is that there are such extremes of experience and such vehemence in declaring what is right or wrong, that I can't help feeling we have altered God's original intention of sending the Holy Spirit in the first place.

A few years ago my sister sent our three children hand-knitted jumpers, made by the hand-knitter next door, as presents.

Vicky, the eldest, tries on her jumper: fits perfectly.

Joe, the middlest, tries on his jumper: fits perfectly.

Sam, the youngest, tries on his jumper: too small.

Had it been Vicky's or Joe's, then one of the others could have had it later. But as it is Sam's and there are no more Smiths on the way, failing the purchase of a pet monkey, the jumper is useless. So we give it away.

Sister rings up: 'How were the jumpers?'

Do I lie?

Do I act like a politician and talk about wool sales?

Or do I tell the truth?

On this occasion I went for option Number 3.

Sister takes it amazingly well and asks for his measurements again: she will get another made.

This we do. However, with past experience, we decide to add a couple of inches so as to make sure it definitely won't be too small this time.

Sister takes measurements, goes next door and gives them to the hand-knitter. However, with past experience, sister decides to add a couple of inches so as to make sure it definitely won't be too small this time.

Next-door hand-knitter commences jumper. However, with past experience he decides to add a couple of inches so as to make sure it definitely won't be too small this time.

By the time the hand-knitting arrives back with us, the jumper is more like an outdoor jacket for an aeroplane than a piece of clothing for a two-year-old.

What's that got to do with the Holy Spirit?

I think we have done the same with the Holy Spirit. The ideas all started from the Bible, but got mixed up with experience, so we have ended up with a contorted interpretation which fits in some places but is blown out of proportion in many others.

Without undertaking a detailed Bible study at this point, let me summarise my understanding of the Holy Spirit.

> The Holy Spirit is God.
>
> Jesus, who is also God, sent the Holy Spirit from the Father (John 15:26) to help us live our lives for God while we are still in our earthly bodies.
>
> God can do anything.

The Holy Spirit can do anything.

I can do anything with the Holy Spirit driving me.

See. Simple, isn't it?

In the Bible there are over seven hundred references to the Holy Spirit, or the Spirit of God, and not one of them mentions going to the front of the church, having people put their hands on you, falling over and screeching like a hungry lion.

So what does this tell me?

It tells me that if this were the only way to receive the Holy Spirit, it would have been made a little clearer. This doesn't mean to say that if you *do* go forward, have some hands put on you, fall over and screech like a lion, you have not had the power of God sweep into your life and change you from that moment onwards.

Let me just say this again, because some of you will not have read the last paragraph the way it was written.

You *can* go to the front of your church, you *can* have people put their hands on you, and you *can* fall over and screech like a lion. As a result of such an experience, the power of God *has* come into your life again and changed you from that moment on.

But it is not the *only* way and, in my opinion, it is not the *most frequently experienced* way.

Frankly, I don't care what happens at the front of the church, how you fall, what comes out of your mouth or whether you speak in tongues. What I care about is the difference the experience makes on Monday morning.

What difference does the power of God make when you read the Bible and see that your life has to change? What difference does it make when, having had an encounter with God, you fail your A levels, your mother is dying, you're being bullied, your partner packs you in, you can't get into the university you wanted, or you have been side-stepped at work?

I know too many people who fall over on Sunday and then talk about it all week to their Christian mates; come Sunday, down they go again. Has it made any difference to their sleeping with their boyfriend or girlfriend, to their relationships with their parents, to their attitude to evangelism or to the poor?

Mind you, there are just as many people still standing who sleep with their partners, trash their parents, keep evangelism a secret and ignore the poor.

The point?

It's not the falling over or the standing up; it's the willingness to let God do anything with you by the Holy Spirit.

In 1994, Devon Malcolm, one of England's fastest bowlers at the time, was playing against South Africa.

Being a fast bowler means that he wasn't much good with the bat. That's something else I have never understood. When I was at school, if a student could swing a bat successfully they could also bowl a wicked ball. The pros, however, only seem to be able to do one or the other. Potentially the subject of another great book!

Still, enough of my questions. Malcolm comes into bat after our excellent batsmen have done the business. Remember Malcolm is a bowler, not a batsman. Given this situation, a South African bowler, who shall remain nameless (because I can't remember), bowls a ball that a first-class batsman who has been in for two days and is about to make his treble century would struggle with. This ball smashes Malcolm on the head.

I don't know if Devon was upset – he didn't mention it on the BBC – but shortly afterwards he and the rest of the England team were all out.

Now, if you know anything about cricket, you will know that, as a consequence of the England team being out, it follows that the South African team were about to go in. Remember, it is not until each one gets out that they are all out, so then they all go in.

You should also be aware that there are eleven people in a cricket team, but you only have to get ten of them out for the whole team to be out.

The innings proceeds, and Devon Malcolm bowls as he has never bowled before. He ends up taking nine of the South African wickets. The commentators are saying that these are Malcolm's best ever figures in a test match; they have never seen him bowl like this in his life.

I don't know whether Devon is a Christian; I have never got close enough to him to ask. But, as a result of his being hit on the head, he was so fired up he came in and demolished the South African batting. I am sure that, as a bowler, every time he played in a test match it was his desire to wipe out the opposition's batting with every ball he bowled. But, as a result of being smashed in the head, Malcolm bowled like he had never bowled before nor since.

I guess because Malcolm wasn't recognised as being a Christian, it wasn't perceived that he had been anointed with Holy Spirit power. Consequently, the idea of smashing people on the head with a cricket ball has never really taken off in church. But it certainly stimulated Malcolm into action.

I don't care if you fall over, get smashed on the head, get prayed for quietly at the back of the church or just meet with Jesus on your own. Whatever your preferred way, once you have done it, get up and do something.

The Holy Spirit is not with us to make us feel soft and warm inside, although sometimes that may be needed.

The Holy Spirit is the force of God in our lives to act.

As Billy Graham once said, 'I don't care how you get it, just get it.'

And if Billy Graham says it, that's good enough for me.

The truth is, we may have something, but it certainly isn't the force of God in our lives to act.

In my visits to other parts of the world, one aspect has been common wherever I go. I meet great people. I meet those who have so much less than I do in what they own materially, but who have so much more in faith and in trusting God. As you talk with them, so many of them are full of vision and of what God is going to do in their lives. They don't deny that life is hard, but their attitude is 'For me to live is Christ and to die is gain'. They realise that God has put them 'in' and one day God will take them 'out'. When they are 'out', they will then be 'in' with God until eternity ends. Until then, they are 'in', and they are 'in' for God.

As a consequence, you find people living and acting in the power of God. Their reality of being filled with the Spirit reaches beyond Sunday, from Monday to Saturday. Their experience is of a life of miracles and an understanding that the reward God has promised is not for here, but for when they will eventually be 'in'.

What are *we* going to do with the power of God while we have the chance?

8 IT'S OK, I'M PRAYING ABOUT IT

When Sue and I ran the youth group at church, we used to end up on Sunday night asking everybody what they wanted to pray for. We would write all their suggestions down on slips of paper, put them in the collection bag and then go round the group. Each person would take out a piece of paper and commit themselves to pray for the subject noted on it all that week.

One night we were up to the part of the routine where people put their hands in the bag to pick the pieces of paper. I get to Gwinderlin (made-up name to protect the misinformed), who tells us she can't take one this week because she is about to go away on holiday and won't be back until Saturday...

Prayer is obviously a simpler subject to tackle than the Holy Spirit. There is only one side to this coin. We all know that we should pray more – nobody would claim that they pray enough – and that we should just get on with it.

But what do we pray for?

I had to prepare a talk to give at a church on 'Why I believe in prayer'. A great subject, because it wasn't about why anyone else should believe in prayer, but why *I* believed in prayer.

As I was preparing, different thoughts were coming to my mind...

Situation One. For several years, in June, a church

day out was organised for the many evangelical churches in the Essex area. The event was a big outdoor affair, with side-stalls, a main attraction in the centre of the field, canoeing, knock-out competitions, finishing with a celebration in a barn in the evening. It was generally a good fun-day-out, not specifically evangelistic although friendship evangelism took place, I'm sure.

I remember going to my church prayer-meeting in May, and one of the offered subjects for prayer was that we have good weather for this fun day.

What a stupid thing to pray for. As if anybody was going to want a lousy thunderstorm with a few hailstones thrown in, along with gale-force winds and subzero temperatures. God knows that, to make the most of the day, folks are going to want good weather. So if God is a God of love, and he loves us to have a good time now and again, then surely we can expect him to give us a bit of a heatwave on the day.

The trouble with this argument is that, without the prayer, we are not showing our dependency on God. If you just expect God to do something and never actually ask for it, then you are taking him for granted. So it is good to pray, I'm told, even if God knows what we want and wants to give it to us without asking, because we are admitting our dependence.

So we prayed for good weather.

I remember the day vividly. Our church organised a bus to take us there. A bus is great because you can all chat and relax, and only one person has the headache of driving. The disadvantage of a bus is that you all have to go at the same time and come home at the same time. You try keeping three children under the age of five happy when there are lousy thunderstorms all around, with a few hailstones thrown in for good measure, not to mention the gale-force winds and subzero temperatures.

Yes, you guessed it – our prayers were *not* answered. However, we were not put off by our total failure to get a result. May came round again and the same prayer was repeated, obviously in the hope of making a greater impression on God.

Situation Two. A friend was going through a very hard time with his wife, who was experiencing extensive depression. One day, after some time, this friend said something like this to his home group: 'I would like to thank you all for your prayers for my wife and I. They haven't made a blind bit of difference, but thanks anyway.'

The group was in uproar. Not probably to his face, because that's not very British, but behind his back they were furious. How could he say such a thing?

If they'd bothered to ask him, he would probably have had plenty of answers for them. The cold facts were that, whether you believed him or not, his wife was no better though many had prayed.

Situation Three. I can think of two people in our church who had cancer in the past. We prayed for them both with great expectations. I even remember one of the leadership team standing up in front of the church and saying that he believed one of them would get better. Both died.

This brings to mind John Wimber, potentially one of the world's best known prayer-warriors for healing, who himself died of cancer.

Pondering on these situations, I had to consider why I believed in prayer. Before my preparation session, I had sat down and prayed for God's message, as I always do, and these were the thoughts God was bringing to my mind. I couldn't help wondering if he was bringing them to my mind for a purpose. What did God want to say that night?

I was sitting at the dining room table. Sue was out, and Sam and Joe were playing elsewhere in the house. However, it has to be said, they were not playing their best: they had interrupted me several times. I am a long-suffering, loving father, with the patience of a retired saint, but I could feel myself getting agitated. Then I had the following conversation with Joe:

Joe: What can we play now, Daddy?

(Having asked this about five times in the last four minutes.)

Daddy: What about Batman and Robin?

Joe: Great idea!

(Peace for about one minute, give or take a minute. Then both boys return…)

Joe: I can't find my Batman mask.

Daddy: Well, you have the shoes, the cape, the trousers, the T-shirt. I'm sure Sam won't forget who you are.

Joe: No, Daddy, I must have the Batman mask.

Daddy: Mummy will be in soon. She will know exactly where the mask is. She always does.

(Isn't it funny how there is always one member of the family who knows exactly where everything is, and it's never you.)

Joe: No, Daddy, Mummy will be ages!

Daddy: *(In a very calm voice)* Right, lets go upstairs and have a look.

See how in control I am, not giving in to a potential tantrum!

We go upstairs. I figure the boys' room is the best place to look, as I can't imagine Sue having used it last, but you never know. We look in the toy box, the dressing-up box, the Lego box, the Duplo box, the shoebox with the soldiers in – you name a box, we have it, and we looked in it.

Joe: Daddy, I know who will know where it is.

Daddy: Yes, so do I, but she's not here right now.

Joe: No, not Mummy – Jesus!

Daddy: Well, you had better pray and ask Jesus then.

Joe: Dear Jesus, please...

While he is praying, I am thinking, *Now what do I do when he has finished praying and we still have to wait for Sue to come to the rescue. I want to teach my children that they should pray, but they are going to be disappointed on this one. Perhaps if I pray after he has prayed, I can drag it out until I hear the car come back and Sue will be the answer.*

Joe: ...A-men.

He opens his eyes, I open mine, Sam opens his, and there is the mask. Guess where. On top of a box.

Somewhat relieved to get the positive side to prayer, I return to the dining-room table to continue, convinced that God has just spoken to me. My thoughts then go to answered prayer, of the times when we prayed for good weather and we had good weather, of the times when we prayed for people with cancer and they have been healed, of the times when people I know had depression and are no longer in depression.

Now I'm totally confused. Why are some prayers answered and some not?

I was at another prayer event, this time a prayer breakfast at a church in the town. We all munched through a great breakfast, sat and considered the items we had to pray for, then split into small groups. I was with one person I knew and there were three others – two were women and one bloke. So, to recap and for your complete understanding, I am in a group of five – two females and three gents.

Prayer commences with the man I don't know. He starts off very quietly, as you do at these events because there are loads of other groups praying. Slowly, this hum of prayer begins to grow. After a while, this man is still praying. As time goes on, he starts to get a bit worked up. You now begin to sense emotion breaking out in this man's prayer. You can tell how emotional he is getting because the more emotional he gets, the louder he becomes. Soon he is shouting at the top of his voice, while all the other groups are still humming.

Some of you have been here before. There is an unwritten code that even if World War Three is breaking out, you keep on praying and nobody looks up. However, intrigued to know if we are going to have to call an ambulance or not, I look up. The friend I've come with has got his hand on this guy's shoulder – I presume to reassure him that everything is OK. But, as to be expected, I look round the rest of the room and the remainder are all carrying on, totally oblivious to the explosion coming from our side of the room.

Eventually he finishes, and so does the rest of the prayer, and slowly everybody is rising from their bowed state. Now I know that within the next minute everyone is going to have a sneaky glance in our direction to see who was doing all the shouting. Given that there were two women in the group and it definitely wasn't a woman's shout, that leaves a choice of the three of us men. This means that there is a one in three chance people are thinking it was me. So I'm sitting there with my hands behind my head in a clasped fashion, one finger protruding outwards, pointing at this guy, just so that I don't get the blame.

So, I wonder, is the reason my prayers don't get answered sometimes because I don't shout loud enough?

If sometimes the answer to our prayers is 'Yes' and sometimes the answer is 'No', what determines which answer we get? Is it the way we pray, or the persistence of our prayers, or the wording of our prayers, or the determination of God?

Years ago, good church people would pray very wordy prayers and conclude, 'If it be your will.'

I remember reading Terry Waite's book, all about his time in captivity. There was an occasion when he and the Archbishop of Canterbury were in Africa and about to go up in a small plane. Before the plane took off, the pilot said that he would like to pray. He concluded with the phrase, 'If it be your will.' The Archbishop remarked that he was grateful for the prayer but would have preferred a slightly more positive attitude.

Like it or not, it does appear to me that God's will has been done, despite the prayers of faithful people. It seems to me that prayer is more about the communication between God and us than it is about the end result.

If we talk about a having a relationship with God, how does this happen?

I can live with a person, wash their socks, make their dinners, iron their underpants, wash their car and clean their toilet, but if I never talk to them I have no relationship. All I am is an unpaid servant. Relationship only begins when talking commences.

On the other hand, there are people whose socks I have never washed; I have never cooked them a dinner; I have never ironed their underpants; they don't have a car;

and their toilet is filthy. But I have a relationship because we talk together and enjoy each other's company.

With God, our main source of communication is through prayer. I wonder if the freedom of prayer is that it is a facility given to us by God to let us have a relationship with him without the medium of a priest; and the result of our conversations is actually only secondary to the main purpose of relationship.

Look at the prayer Jesus gave us, which many have learnt off by heart (Matt 6:9–13; Luke 11:2–4). Although it has its benefits as a recited poem, this prayer is probably better treated as a series of headings for us to ad lib. If we were to follow it through on this basis, we would start with praise – a good place to begin when talking to the Creator. We then move on to asking for our basic needs. Many don't have to bother with this any more because we go out, earn money and get a salary at the end of the month. But it's there as a backup should we ever be made redundant.

After our basic needs, we ask God to do his stuff now as one day it will be done in heaven. If we stop and think about it, this really means that we are asking him what he wants us to do. Consequently, it's not wise to spend too much time praying for this. If you are not careful, God might give you a task to do which will take time away from earning the daily bread (although he has already promised that he will provide our daily bread). In any case, it doesn't reflect reality: in heaven we will have eternity to do what God wants and, presumably, bodies which don't need feeding; but while we are here, we have bodies to feed and only a little time.

Then we confess.

And then we finish with thanks again.

Jesus doesn't suggest we go to God with our daily request sheets. I think he is encouraging us to talk with

God and thus build a relationship. The more time we spend talking to God, the more we will understand, the more we will know what to do, the more we will see God's will being done on earth.

Several years ago, when the Rwanda crisis hit the headlines in the UK, I was in church for family prayers. Those leading the prayers explained to God where Rwanda was, the atrocities that were taking place, the fact their information came from Thursday's News at Ten, and the problems the church were facing in Rwanda. They concluded by asking God to do something.

Now call me an old traditionalist, but I think God already knew about Rwanda and the state of the church. Given that he put Rwanda there in the first place, he probably knew where it was. I am sure thousands of people can't get slaughtered without God knowing about it, because it's the devil doing what he does best. But it is always important to give your sources when talking to God, just so he can double-check.

Where I think God was probably a little confused was when the prayer concluded with the request that he do something.

Do something?!!!

'I have given you the Holy Spirit. What more do you want? You are my last hope. You have had your eyes opened to what evil men are doing. And you are asking me to do something? Get up off your prayer-stools and be the people you could be if you would just let the Holy Spirit rip through your life!'

I believe in a God of miracles, but if you look at the Bible and at history the majority of the miracles were acted out through people. God has chosen to work through people. Strange as this may seem, that means you and me. If you like, God needs a body to work through. But if the body says no, then God doesn't do his work.

Prayer is great and essential to our relationship with God, but prayer is about our getting direction to do stuff rather than our praying that someone else will do it.

When we pray for God to do something, what do we really think we are asking for? That he will send an extraterrestrial to Rwanda to sort it all out?

When we pray for money, where do we expect it to come from? Will God just send an envelope full of money through the sky and into our postman's bag for delivery to our door? Does God really have every currency waiting by his fingertips so that when we ask, he just sends it off?

No. If I need money for whatever reason, God motivates some disciple somewhere who has excess money; they become aware of my need and they put a cheque in the post.

Likewise, when somebody is starving or uneducated or malnourished or cold. When we pray that they will be helped, what happens?

A Marks and Spencer meal floats out the sky?

A few sheep get together and make a jumper?

No.

Somebody somewhere does something.

Who's it going to be?

9 THE CALL

There's no one on his deathbed says,
'I wish I'd spent more time in the office.'

Many are under the impression that the church is totally out of date and living in a past era. If you go into school and brainstorm a class on the word 'church', you get:

Boring, stained-glass windows, vicars, hats, flowers...

The majority of people saying these things have never set foot inside a church, with the exception of their christening and they obviously didn't pay a lot of attention that day!

For some churches the above is probably true, but many have made extensive efforts to try to update their image:

Heavy wooden doors are replaced by smoked glass.

Friendly people meet you at the smoked glass-door.

Hard wooden pews are replaced by plastic seats.

There's carpet on the floor.

Cold lofty buildings are replaced by schoolrooms.

Best suits and frocks are no longer expected.

A full band replaces the pipe organ.

The preacher tells jokes.

Modern language Bibles are provided.

And there's coffee and tea at the end.

The one thing that still does not seem to have changed is that nobody ever sits down – we all have to be 'seated'.

Another constant from the days of Abraham right up to tomorrow is that before we get up off our bums and do something, we have to have a 'call'.

This, of course, only applies to certain parts of our lives. We don't generally wait for a call to go to the toilet. We eat when we get hungry, if there is food available. We go to school and further education if we are capable. We get a job and earn money if the economic climate is OK. We spend just a little bit more than our income is, regardless of our level of remuneration. We go on holiday.

But if it means doing something 'For God', we need a call.

We love it when we see others get 'the call,' and we thank God we didn't.

To ensure that 'the call' is right first time, we have certain control strings to protect us against premature action.

Praying about a particular issue for several years is a favourite and one I have used myself on many occasions. Who can argue with you if your inactivity is backed up by 'I'm praying about it'.

Another favourite is looking for signs. I remember a story of somebody putting a five-pound note in a book before going to bed and praying that if God wanted him to do X, he must move the five pounds to a different page by the following morning. In the morning, once awoken, the guy dived out of bed, picked up the book, and there was the five-pound note still in the same place. Relieved, he fell back into bed to sleep off the tension. When questioned about this later, our five-pound inserter stated that he didn't believe himself that the five pounds would move, but if God can do anything then it was possible.

Adrian Plass, I think, highlights the credulity given to such practices as these with this ironic prayer: 'If an alien and a midget knock at the door in the next five minutes, then I will go anywhere for you, God!' Blow me down, three minutes later the mother-in-law and her dog turn up. But still that isn't seen as a sign. (I added the mother-in-law bit.)

Another practice similar to the above is what we rather quaintly call 'laying down a fleece'. This originated in the Bible with a guy called Gideon who, by all accounts, was a bit of a weed. God asked him to lead armies against fearsome enemies, so Gideon retreats to bed in his tent. But before he zips up the door he leaves a rug, otherwise known as a fleece, just outside. He then prays that if God *really* wants him to lead armies, when he wakes up in the morning the fleece should be dry and all the grass around it wet.

Gideon wakes up in the morning and, sure enough, there is dew all on the grass and the rug is bone-dry.

So then he tries the five-pound trick. The next night he prays that the rug will be wet and the grass will be dry. Wakes up in the morning and all is as he requested.

To bring these examples up to date and in line with our modern culture, they could be adapted slightly and then applied to our situation. The result might look like this.

You go to bed at night, look out of the window and ask God, 'If you really want me to work with the homeless, turn my car on the roof by the morning and leave all the others upright.'

Next morning comes and you rush to the window

and some drunken hooligans from the local club have come down the street and, of all the cars to turn over, they have chosen yours.

Was that an answer to prayer?

Anyway, to be totally biblical, the following night comes.

You go to bed, look out of the window and ask God, 'If you really want me to work with the homeless, turn every other car in the street on its roof by the morning and leave mine upright.'

Next morning comes and you rush to the window.

Drunken hooligans! How much did they have to drink to turn that many cars on their roofs?

Fortunately for you, yours is still on its roof from the previous evening so, thankfully, the sign hasn't been fulfilled. But that was close...

The trouble is, we want everything signed, sealed and delivered in a watertight package.

Why?

Well, it's either selfishness or pride.

Selfishness because we don't really want to do what God wants. Pride because we can't bear the thought of sticking our necks out and getting it wrong and have everyone judging us. While we dot the i's cross, the t's, bend the s's, cap the e's, curve the b's and zig the zeds, thirteen million people continue to exist as refugees.

I was at a seminar recently where the speaker described the following experience. A man owned a garage, full access to which was obstructed by a telegraph pole. For years the owner lived with this, using the restricted access available. Then, one day, enough was enough. He decided to remove the pole (I assume it was an out-of-use pole).

On the other side of the courtyard there was another

out-building which needed to be avoided when the pole fell to the ground. So the owner asked somebody else to cut the pole for him. Meanwhile, he clambered onto the roof of the garage and tied a rope round himself and the pole to prevent its free, uncontrolled fall causing unwanted damage.

The cutting commenced. The owner braced himself on top of the garage. All was going to plan. The point came when the strength in the pole keeping it upright became weaker than the force on the pole pulling it to the ground. It also became apparent that the weight and momentum of the falling pole was in excess of the weight and stability of the owner on the roof. Without warning, the pole proceeded in the direction of the out-building, with the garage owner flying closely behind. Unfortunately for him, due to the precision, dedication and commitment given to tying himself to the pole, there was no quick release. Consequently, with that same commitment, he followed the pole fully to its eventual destination, the out-building.

The final comment from the storyteller was that life is not a precise science. Sometimes things go well and sometimes they don't. Sometimes we pray about situations and God knows it's not going to work, but he sits back and has a good laugh when the poles hit the ground.

Why is it that we have to have guidance so tightly sewn up?

Peter, a fisherman friend of Jesus, takes a lot of stick from preachers and others who think they understand the Bible. He is often described as the one who opens his mouth first and engages brain at some point in the future. The bit where the disciples are in the boat and Jesus is out walking on the water is no exception.

The story goes that Peter looks out over the sea and

sees what he thinks is a ghost, even though, like a good churchgoer of my parent's generation, he didn't believe in them. Then he wipes his glasses and realises that it might be Jesus walking on the water. So typical Peter shouts, 'Jesus, if that is you, tell me to come to you.'

Jesus says, 'Hi, Peter, it's me. Come on in, the water's great.'

Peter gets out of the boat and starts to walk.

Next – well, only what we expect from Peter – he takes his eyes off Jesus, looks at the size of the waves and thinks, *You have got to be having a laugh!*

And he starts to sink.

Then the preachers continue, with their superior attitude, to explain that Peter's heart was in the right place but, oh dear, he took his eyes off Jesus and started to sink. Of course, you know that's what happens to us when we take our eyes off the Lord. Preach over.

Ian Henderson of Viz-A-Viz takes a slightly different view. Ian goes a little further, as he tends to do. Ian says, 'I wonder what the conversation at breakfast was the next morning?'

There are the disciples, frying up a few fish on the beach, reflecting on what happened the night before, impressed by yet another surprise about Jesus. Everyone is a little dumbstruck. Then Peter says, 'I walked on water last night!'

'You didn't?!'...

Thank you, Ian Henderson.

He's got a point hasn't he? We all tend to concentrate on the bit where Peter stopped looking at Jesus and sank. *But he, and only he, walked on the water.* Nobody else bothered to get out of the boat. Nobody else sank, because nobody else saw the point of getting their feet wet.

Most of us are so concerned about sinking that we

never get around to stepping out of the boat. That's why we have to be sure. Because if we are going to be daring enough to step out of the boat, we need to be certain that we are going to walk and walk a long way. We are not going to get caught out with this sinking lark. After all, it will ruin our shoes.

Tony Campolo talks of a visit he made to Haiti. While there, he met some fifty children who were orphaned, hungry, without education, without medical care, without hope. He went home to the States and he visited a few of his friends. He told them about these children and he told them what he wanted to do. He wanted to build a home, provide houseparents, feed them, give them an education, provide medical care and give these children a hope. He told his friends that this was going to cost a lot of money and he was asking them to give it to him.

They did.

Campolo says, 'I had no call.

'I simply saw hurting children who needed somebody to help them, and I knew I could.

'There was no call.'

I attended a seminar once at a venue designed to hold about one hundred people. Unfortunately, about a hundred and twenty people turned up, the consequence being that we were somewhat crammed in, although a seat was found for everyone.

It was a relatively cold day but, as you know, when a hundred and twenty people get inside a room designed to hold a hundred, slowly the accumulated body heat of the participants begins to raise the temperature of the room. I was sitting at the back and overheard the stewards, Harold and Gwynith, talking.

Harold says to Gwynith, 'I think we should open a couple of windows.' Gwynith scurries off and discreetly opens the two windows nearest the back.

About five minutes later, Harold says to Gwynith, 'I think we should open a couple of windows near the front.' Gwynith scurries off and discreetly opens two windows near the front.

About four minutes later, Harold says to Gwynith, 'I think we should open every window you possibly can.' Gwynith scurries off and discreetly opens every possible window she can open.

About three minutes later, Harold realises that the heat is rising quicker than Gwynith can open windows. Harold says to Gwynith, 'I think we should open the doors at the back here.' Gwynith scurries off to open the doors, only to realise she has scurried past them, so she comes back and opens the back doors.

About two minutes later, Harold says to Gwynith, 'I think we should open the doors at the front, to get a through draft.' Gwynith scurries off to open the doors at the front as discreetly as possible.

About one minute later, Harold says to Gwynith, 'I don't know what else to do!'

To which Gwynith replies, 'Do you think it would help if we switched off the heating?'

Why is it we think of the most obvious things last?

We would far sooner pray than do anything. We would rather wait for 'a call' than build a home for starving children. We would rather tell everybody else that something should be done before we put our hands in our own pockets.

Tony Campolo continues his story by explaining how he facilitated the building of a home for fifty children. On the day of the opening, a bus was laid on to go out to the villages to a specific place to collect the fifty children and bring them back to their new home. Campolo sent the word out for the fifty children to meet at the collection point. A party was organised and the day set.

Campolo went to the collection point as arranged, excited at the prospect that fifty starving, sick, homeless, uneducated children were going to be shown the love of Jesus and have a hope for the future. However, to his horror, when they get to the meeting place there were not the fifty children he had built the home for, but three hundred. He explains how he then had the job of choosing fifty children, knowing that he was basically leaving the other two hundred and fifty to die without hope. But Campolo says, 'I had to choose fifty, because that was all I had room for.'

With the fifty chosen, they made their way back to the home where the party began. As they got out of the bus, a little choir was singing:

God is so good,
God is so good,
God is so good,
He's so good to me.'

As the words hit Campolo's ears, anger raged within his mind against God.

If God really was that good, then they wouldn't have just left two hundred and fifty children to die in the villages. As this torment raged in his mind, he felt Jesus speak to him.

'Tony, I *am* good. But there are people down there who call themselves Christians who don't let me have control of their lives.'

Tony concludes that we will only care as much as we are prepared to submit our lives to the will of Jesus. Is he right?

We do not have to wait for a call to realise that there

is great need all around us, both here on our doorsteps and overseas. Whether it be homeless people in the inner cities, starvation in Africa, child abuse, support for single mothers, assistance for the elderly or... There are so many people needing love and support. And what are we doing? We are waiting for a call. Well, treat this book as a call if you want to. Or is that not quite how you wanted it?

There is a town on the Essex coast called Frinton. It is a place where the modern world has passed by without it noticing. The planners have managed to keep out amusement arcades, pubs, paying car parks, large out-of-town supermarkets and chewing gum. It is a great place where little shops can still make money and you can walk down the High Street without getting gum on your shoes. It won't cost you a fortune in slot machines to enjoy a day at the beach, and there are no traffic wardens.

As you walk along the front there are, at very regular intervals, wooden benches with people's names inscribed on them. I don't know whether it is because the named people sat down on these benches and died there, or they died somewhere else and the bench was put up in their memory. But I think it's rather sad that all that remains to commemorate them is something which is sat on by people who have no idea who they were.

I hope when I die I will be commemorated by more than a bit of wood people sit on and dogs pee against. I hope when I die someone somewhere will remember me because I did something with the time and the money I have been given to help make the lives of others better. I hope when I die somebody else might be alive because I *did* something rather than just thought about it.

I sincerely hope people don't say, 'He didn't do much, but he was waiting for a...'

10 EXCEPTIONS TO EVERY RULE?

There was a man called Elijah. Some would say there *is* a man called Elijah, because according to records he never died, he just disappeared. That would make him about three thousand years old. Call me an old traditionalist, but I can't imagine meeting anybody three thousand years old walking down the high street to pay his gas bill.

Enough of that. Elijah lived at a time when the majority of the people in the country where he lived had rejected God and were worshipping anything but God. People were having sex with whoever they felt like and wherever they felt like it. Nobody cared about the poor. Children were being abused. And the leader of the country was leading the way as described above, and nobody was doing anything about it.

The year was 1999.

(No, that was a little joke!)

The king was Ahab who perhaps on his own wasn't such a bad chap, but he was married to an evil woman named Jezebel (Jezzy to her friends) who basically told him what he could and could not do.

To help him, Ahab had a thousand religious representatives on his advisory team. They, however, kept their mouths tightly shut. I guess at one time there were one thousand and one religious advisors. One day one religious guy goes to Ahab and says, 'Excuse me, King, but nobody worships God anymore. There is sex in the streets with anyone you fancy. Nobody is helping the poor. Children are being abused. And you are the worst of all of them.'

Suddenly you have one less religious advisor and one thousand in paid employ keeping their mouths shut.

Along comes Elijah. He sees that everybody is having it away with whoever they want, whether the same sex or otherwise. He sees that nobody cares about the poor. He sees that children are being abused. He sees that nobody goes to church. And he sees that the king is leading the way.

Elijah prays about all this. God speaks to him and tells him to go and tell Ahab that there will be no more rain in the country until everyone is prepared to acknowledge how wrong they are and are ready to come back to church and worship God. So Elijah makes an appointment with the king and, in front of all the king's advisors, he tells him the score.

Now the thousand religious advisors have a problem What do they do now? If they support Elijah, suddenly there will be a thousand less religious wallahs. But if they say Elijah's just a head-case and it stops raining, you'll probably have a thousand less religious wallahs.

Mum's the word

Anyway, nobody pays much attention to this crank from the countryside and life goes on as normal.

The next day, the papers are full of the discourse, with photos of Elijah running away into the distance and religious advisors saying, 'No comment', all over the place.

Picture the scene at the watering-holes the next night. Let's imagine we have two water-hole visitors called Bill and Ben.

(Time: the day after Elijah features in all the papers.)

Bill: Guess what? Some berk stormed into the Houses of Parliament last night saying that he worshipped the only true God and that there'd be no more rain until he say so. What d'ye think of that then?

Ben: Bloke's a raving nutter. Lucky he didn't get arrested and that Jezebel have his head for tea!

(One week later.)

Bill: Guess what? That berk who said that there'd be no rain until he say so, must be right cock-a-hoop.

Ben: Why that be then?

Bill: Because there's been no rain since he say so.

Ben: Bloke's a raving nutter. Just a coincidence!

(One month later.)

Bill: Guess what? That berk who said that there'd be no rain until he say so, must be really right cock-a-hoop now then.

Ben: Why that be then?

Bill: Well, because there's still been no rain since he say so.

Ben: Bloke's a raving nutter. Just a coincidence!

(One year later.)

Bill: Guess what? That berk who said that there'd be no rain until he say so, must be no berk.

Ben: Why that be then?

Bill: Well, because there's *still* been no rain since he say so, for over a year.

Ben: Bloke's a raving nutter. Just a coincidence!

(Three years later.)

Bill: Guess what? That berk who said that there'd be no rain until he say so, he know something we don't.

Ben: What that be then?

Bill: When it going to rain and when it ain't.

Ben: Bloke's a raving weatherman!

After three years without rain, most people realised that perhaps they should listen to Elijah, so he calls the whole country to a contest. Those who worship anything that moves must ask their god to light a fire without matches; he, Elijah, will do the same thing but asking God the Creator.

Surprise, surprise! The false-god worshippers dance all day and nothing happens; Elijah asks God once and a fireball comes down from heaven.

But after this incident Elijah is scared again. Why? Because Jezebel is none too pleased and wants his head for tea (again). So Elijah runs off to commit suicide, which is a little difficult to understand because if he wanted to die he could have saved all the running about and just let Jezebel have the satisfaction.

This story can be read in 1 Kings 17:1 – 19:21. But to get it all, you have to read it all. Funny that.

Throughout the story, from the time that Elijah goes and visits Ahab to the time he has the fire contest, you keep reading that Elijah gets a call from God and there appears to be no hesitation: he just gets up and does whatever God has told him to do. This, of course, is good back-up for the exception to the rule. The key being twofold:

1 That we listen.

2 That when we hear, we do.

Elijah does both.

But there comes a point when Elijah hears the call and doesn't respond. In 1 Kings 19:15–17, after the fire incident is over, God asks him to go and finish the job he has started. God wanted to end the worship of all other gods in the country once and for all, but this couldn't be achieved while Elijah was up in the mountain. God tells Elijah to get three others to do it for him. If you carry on reading 2 Kings 8 – 10, you'll discover that between Elisha, Jehu and Hazael, they eventually destroyed all those leading the worship of other gods. But because they were all busy with their own affairs, nothing actually happened for some twenty to forty years.

What happens when someone says no to God? Well, I'll tell you.

An angel jumps out of the sky, looking something like Arnie with wings, points a treble-barrelled sawn-off laser hooper-scooper at you and makes it quite clear that if you don't do what you're told, he will blast you into the next planet.

Alternatively, somebody else just gets on and does it.

Both answers are about as camp as each other. Arnie ain't got wings and there aren't enough people floating around to do the jobs you can't be bothered doing, because they have jobs of their own to do.

While Elijah didn't do what God asked him to do, nothing got done. God didn't force him and nobody else did it for him – well, not for thirty-odd years and even then it took three of them. The simple truth is that when we say no to God, it don't get done.

But at least Elijah said yes a load more times than most.

The trouble is, there was no original call.

I always used to think that God spoke to Elijah, and Elijah got up and did whatever it was that God wanted him to do. But then one day I was reading the book of James and saw that James reckoned that it was Elijah who prayed there would be no rain and there wasn't. Now we all know who stopped the rain, but it wasn't God who told Elijah to ask God to stop the rain. If we understand James properly, what I think we see is this.

It was *Elijah* who saw all that was wrong. He saw that everybody was worshipping anything that moved. He saw people having it away in the streets. He saw that nobody was being faithful to God. He saw that children were being abused. He could see all of this and he knew it was wrong. So he did something about it. He went to see the king and told him that it wasn't going to rain until he (Elijah) said so. Then Elijah went to God and said it would be handy if it didn't rain any more because he had kind of put his head on the block.

There was no call. Elijah took the initiative. Elijah saw what was wrong. Elijah did something and then prayed.

We have the Holy Spirit, we have brains, we have resources and we know how to make decisions.

Why are we waiting for a call?

11 IS THIS BIBLICAL OR NOT?

Daughter: Dad, can I have a dog?
Dad: No.
Daughter: But Dad, when you were my age you had a dog.
Dad: Things were different then.
Daughter: Aren't things different now?
Dad: No, they're exactly the same.

Why is it important that this book is biblical?

Is it because only those who call themselves Christian can get involved in releasing people from poverty?

Certainly not. However, I do believe that if the only solution we have for a hungry person is to give him a loaf of bread or show him how to make a loaf of bread, then he only has half the answer. As this book has sought to demonstrate, even though the Christian world has let the poor down, if we get motivated enough to act we will have a greater impact than those who have no concept of why Jesus died. I don't expect anyone who's not Christian to agree with that. If you don't see it for your own life, you're never going to see it for the poor.

The reason it's important that what we have been saying here is biblical is because if it is not, all we have are some fine ideals which most would probably agree with, even if they aren't prepared to do anything about them. If it is not biblical, the fact you are not prepared to do anything is no worse than me not doing anything about freeing battery hens: we all have our priorities, and how we prioritise our efforts depends on our personal preference.

But if what is being said here *is* biblical, then those who supposedly live by the Bible need to realise that what has been termed in the past as 'social action' is in fact an integral part of being a disciple.

That phrase 'being a disciple' needs explaining. You will have noticed that often we talk about 'disciples' rather than 'Christians'. This is no mistake: it is my contention that there is a big difference between those who call themselves Christian and those who are disciples. Not everybody who calls themselves Christian is using the same definition.

'People who call themselves Christian' can cover those who were born in England, live upright lives, go to church, don't swear, watch *Songs of Praise* and pray occasionally. But this doesn't make you a disciple.

A disciple is somebody who follows a master, in this case, Jesus. When I say 'follow', I don't mean 'go to the same place'; I mean 'imitates the master', or 'copies'; I mean 'demonstrates his or her discipleship by attempting to stand up for what the master stands for'. Your being born in England no more makes you a disciple than, as Corrie Ten Boom put it, putting a mouse in a cookie jar makes a mouse a cookie.

Or driving a car fast makes you Damon Hill.

Or wearing your shirts the wrong way round makes you a vicar.

Or wearing a tea cosy on your head makes you a teapot.

To my understanding, a disciple is a person who, because Jesus died for them, is living their life in thanks to God for Jesus.

Something we must remember is that I have an ability to make the Bible say what I want it to, which actually is no better than your ability to do the same thing. So how do we understand what the Bible is really saying rather than making it say what we want it to?

Well, this is done by taking an overview of loads of verses and building up the big picture, rather than taking bits in isolation.

Sue and I have a friend whose sister has just got married to her husband (well, who else would she get married to?). Both wife and husband are in the army. The husband has actually been posted to Serbia right now, and since they married about eight months ago they have only spent their honeymoon together and another couple of short breaks.

Our friend, commenting on her sister's situation, said that each time her sister sees her husband it makes the relationship worse.

Taking that sentence in isolation would lead me to conclude that it was better, then, that they didn't see each other! But understanding the conversation in the light of other information about the relationship, I knew that the statement didn't actually mean that their relationship got worse as a result of them seeing each other. What she meant was, their desire to be together increased, which consequently made things worse, if you see what I mean.

The point being that my friend's statement can only be truly understood in the light of other information.

In the book of Luke, Jesus comes out of the closet, so to speak. We read about his birth in a bit of detail; we read about an incident when he is twelve. Other then these, Jesus reaches thirty and doesn't hit the headlines in any way.

Then we get to his baptism and the giving of the Holy Spirit. That's a bit funny because he was conceived by the Holy Spirit, which would suggest that he should have had the Holy Spirit from birth. But there, the subject of another book...

Jesus wanders off into the wilderness for about a month and a half, then comes back and goes to church for what seems like the first time, although I'm sure it wasn't! With his mission now in hand, he makes public what he has come to do by reading from the Old Testament prophet, Isaiah:

The Spirit of the Lord is with me, to:
Bring good news to the poor;
Free prisoners;
Make blind people see;
Free the oppressed;
Tell people about the day of the Lord.

Many today have seen the above as a directive towards the cross; that all the above statements should be read in the context of Jesus coming to *save sinners*. The poor, therefore, are those who don't know God; the captives are those captured by sin; the blind are those who see no need for God; the oppressed are those weighed down by the pressure of sin; and 'the day of the Lord' is when Jesus is coming back.

But that isn't exactly what Jesus said. He said that he came to bring good news to the poor, free those who are captives, make blind people see and free the oppressed. Then finally, he says, he is here to tell of the day when the Lord will come back.

If we who call ourselves disciples – which means 'followers of our master' – are doing what Jesus did, then what 'good news' have we given to the poor? Because it doesn't seem to me that they are getting much 'good news'.

It is *our* responsibility to bring good news to the poor. Not just for one day far away, when mortal things will end and eternal things will be eternal, but good news that is good news *now*.

So as not to fall into my own trap of picking out isolated verses, I have gone through the book of Luke and listed some of the events which point towards discipleship being about a simple lifestyle, caring for the sick and sharing what's ours:

1:48	Mary sings of being a simple servant.
1:53	She states that God has fed the hungry…
1:53	And the rich are sent away with nothing.
2:7	No room at the inn for Jesus to be born.
3:11	If you have two shirts, give one away…
3:11	And if you have food, share it.
4:35	Jesus makes a man better.
4:39	Jesus makes a woman better.
4:40	Jesus makes everyone better.
5:13	Jesus makes a man better.
5:15	Jesus makes loads more better.
5:24	Jesus makes a man better.
5:28	Levi leaves everything to follow Jesus.
5:32	Jesus says that he has come for the rejects.
6:10	Jesus makes a man better.
6:18	Jesus makes loads more better.
6:20	The poor will be happy because of the kingdom.
6:21	The hungry will be full.
6:21	The tearful will laugh.
6:24	The rich have had their easy life.
6:25	Those who are well-fed now will be hungry.
6:25	Those who are laughing now will cry.
6:29	If someone asks for something, give more.
6:35	Love your enemies.
6:38	Give to others and God will give to you.
6:38	The amount you give others will be the amount God gives you.

7:14	Jesus brings a boy back from the dead.
7:21	Jesus makes loads more better.
8:3	A few women feed Jesus and the disciples.
8:44	Jesus makes a woman better.
8:54	Jesus brings a girl back from the dead.
9:3	Jesus sends disciples out with no resources.
9:6	The disciples make loads better.
9:13–14	Jesus feeds about 20,000 (5,000 men plus their families).
9:23	If you want to follow Jesus, you must leave everything behind.
9:42	Jesus makes a boy better.
10:4	Jesus sends disciples out with no resources.
10:9	Jesus tells disciples to go make folks better.
10:25–37	The good Samaritan.
11:3	Jesus tells us to ask for daily bread.
11:28	You'll be happy if you obey God's teaching.
11:42	You are tithing but neglecting justice.
11:46	What are you doing to help?
12:13–21	Foolish rich man.
12:21	Foolish are those who are rich here but don't know God.
12:22	Don't worry about what you will eat.
12:29	Don't worry about what you will eat.
12:31	Be concerned about the kingdom.
12:33	Sell the lot and give it to the poor.
12:48	If you have a lot, God expects a lot.
13:12	Jesus makes a woman better.
14:7–11	Don't bother about status.
14:13	Give the best to the poor.
14:33	You can't be a disciple unless you give up everything.
16:11	If you can't be trusted with this world's wealth, can you be trusted with kingdom wealth?

16:13	Can't serve money and God.
16:15	Stuff you value is worth nothing to God.
17:14	Jesus makes ten men better.
18:22	Sell all you have and give to the poor.
18:24	It's hard for the rich to go to heaven.
18:28	The disciples left their homes to follow Jesus.
18:43	Jesus makes a man better.
19:8	Zacchaeus is willing to give it all away.
19:30	Jesus borrows a donkey because he doesn't have his own.
20:47	Don't rob widows.
21:2	The widow with her little gives so much more.
20:34	Don't overeat.
22:26	Roles will be reversed.
22:63	Jesus is mocked and beaten.
23:32	Jesus dies with a couple of thieves.
23:50–53	Jesus borrows another's burial plot.
24:47	Go everywhere and tell everyone.

Now I appreciate that I have missed some, and I also understand that there are some which, we could argue, are taken out of context. (For example, take the penultimate reference, 23:50–53: if Jesus had had his own tomb it would, I must confess, have been a little extravagant of him, given that he was only in it for three days. Much better value for money to borrow somebody else's.) But for these few contentious items, I think that the above list gives a general picture of how one of the Gospel writers depicts the life of Jesus.

Could I also point out that tithing is only mentioned once in Luke? And even then it is coupled with a telling-off for hypocrisy, when Jesus has a go at the Pharisees because they are tithing but remaining wilfully ignorant about doing justice and loving God.

May I also point out that swearing isn't mentioned at

all? Once at home-group, somebody got right into one about a so-called Christian who swore: the argument went that the person in question *knowingly* swore and therefore could not possibly be a Christian. Now I bet there are loads of people who feel fairly pleased with themselves that they don't swear but who have never bothered to find out that, in the list of biblical priorities, especially in Luke's opinion, it is hardly the number one item.

There is absolutely no reference to earning as much as you can, spending most on yourself and giving what you have left over. This, however, is how many in the West live.

Why so hot on some things and so neglectful of others?

I was travelling in the car one night. Inside the car were just me and a flask of tea. And I did a really stupid thing. I tried to open the flask *and* drink the tea as I was driving along (not biblical, I know). I slowly came to the conclusion that I was never actually going to be able to pour a cup of tea into the cap, so I decided to have a go at drinking it straight from the flask. The problem was, given that it was dark, I couldn't actually see inside the flask. Consequently, when I put it to my lips my only way of knowing that I was about to get a mouthful of tea depended on the flow of hot steam coming out of the end. If you have never adopted this method of tea drinking, you must try it some time.

Anyway, I negotiated my first mouthful rather well. I was attempting the trick with a little more confidence the second time – my senses told me I was close to getting to the tea – when I hit a small divot in the road. In an instant, my careful negotiations were wasted as the flask lurched in my hand. I ended up with a bit more tea than I bargained for. It shot out the end of the flask, all over me, all over the car, all over anything that was in the front of the car. I gave up, put the lid back on and travelled to my destination, damp and just hoping that the dampness wasn't going to result in too obvious a stain.

The trouble with looking too closely at the Bible is that you get a bit more than you bargained for.

What we all have to remember is that we have been taught the Bible by people who have already reached a conclusion on how to live by it, and they pass their conclusions on to us. But if they have got it wrong, we get it wrong. If you attempted to read the Bible as though it were an academic history book, you might find it easier to understand. The trouble is, when attempting to understand the Bible we are always trying to make it fit with how we live. So we need to read it, reach our conclusions and then apply them to our lives.

Having given a brief overview of Luke, I now want to take a couple of other verses which I hope, given the above, I will not be accused of taking out of context.

At the end of Matthew, those who thought they had the law sussed were arguing that if they had seen Jesus hungry or unclothed, then they would have fed him and clothed him; but they didn't, so they never had the opportunity to demonstrate their 'heart for the poor'. Jesus turned round and said to them that whenever they ignored *anyone* in need, they ignored him. It is as if the needy were himself but they did nothing (25:45).

Have we got that? If we ignore the cry of just one person who needs food or clothing, or is being mistreated or sick or lonely, it is as though we ignore Jesus. That's just one. This must mean that if there is one starving child left, then we have left Jesus to starve.

In Acts, we read about the early church – the group of people who, having spent three years with Jesus, were now attempting to follow on where he left off.

What do we see? I'll tell you.

We see them meeting together, taking communion, doing miracles and sharing what they had with those who did not have (Acts 2:42–47). Their numbers grew daily. None of them went without. Not only did they share what was in their pockets but, if there was a particular need, someone would go and sell something in order to provide for it.

Does that sound like the church you go to? Then maybe we don't go to church anymore. Perhaps we go to some man-made structure, but *church* it is not.

I appreciate that two thousand years later you can't still have new people being added daily, because if the model had continued, there would be nobody left to add. But my church doesn't look like the one Luke talks about.

I want to finish with one more verse, then you can go and get your tea or coffee, and I believe there may be biscuits.

1 John 4:20: If we say we love God and hate our brothers and sisters, we are liars.

Need I say more?

Closing remarks

In life you will have noticed that we go through trends of speech. 'Cool', 'wicked', 'pants', 'sucks' are the few that are in at the moment.

'Cool' means good and has nothing to do with temperature.

'Wicked' means cool and has nothing to do with being evil.

'Pants' means 'It's not good' and has nothing to do with underwear.

'Sucks' means 'pants' and has nothing to do with a baby's bottle.

In church it's the same, with words like 'share', 'minister', 'worship', 'heart for the poor'.

'Share' means talk and has nothing to do with giving away anything physical.

'Minister' means something you do to someone and has nothing to do with the guy up front.

'Worship' means singing songs and has nothing to do with lifestyle.

'Heart for the poor' means you say the right words but do nothing.

Because I wander around talking for Tearfund, people know where I'm coming from and what will please me. I got up in a church once and gave what some felt was a direct word of prophecy for the church. In brief, I said we had closed the curtains on a sunny day and had switched the lights on: I considered that this was a picture of how we had shut out God because we felt that our man-made structures were better.

One of the leadership team came up to me afterwards and said, 'Yes I agree. If we switched the lights off, we could sponsor a child with the money saved!'

I didn't say that, but he thought it would make me happy.

Well, I'm also sick of hearing people who tell me they have a 'heart for the poor' and sit on their pants being cool. Much as God is interested in your heart, he wants more than that: it's your money he wants, it's your effort, it's your energy, it's your risk taking, it's all of that. Not just your bloody heart. Get real, be wicked, stop the talk and do it.

Close to our home is a house, outside of which sits a Ferrari. Every time we drive past that house, we look to see if the Ferrari is there. One day the conversation in the car goes like this:

Joe: Daddy, do you think I will ever have a Ferrari?

Dad: Joe, if you really want a Ferrari and you save all your money and your ambition is to one day own a Ferrari, then I guess one day you will own a Ferrari.

But ... Ferraris are very expensive, and you may find that when you have enough money to buy a Ferrari, actually you want to spend that money on other things, like a house or food or clothes or even giving some to other people.

Joe: Oh, all right then, I'll have a Mini.

We look at our response to the developing world with similar extremes. We realise that a lot needs to be done, we take a look at what we have and think, *Oh, I don't need these designer labels – I'll get rid of them. And this house is too big – we'll live in a smaller one. And hey! who needs carpets when you've got good floorboards? And candles are just as effective as light bulbs. And...*

As we reflect on that extreme, we realise that this is ridiculous. So instead of moving our ideals to having a simpler life, we reject the whole lot and do nothing.

Joe will probably never have a Ferrari or a Mini: he will probably end up with something in between. Christians in this country will never end up living by candlelight on floorboards, and we shouldn't settle for giving away the bare minimum. But will we end up being minimalistic in our attitude to giving to the poor of the world, or will we manage to justify our giving because we don't want to harm our lifestyle?

If we want to make the Bible our 'code for life', we too should aim for somewhere in between.

Friends of ours, incidentally, are on salaries significantly less than the national average.

'Why?' you may ask.

Well, it's because they work for Christian organisations which are funded by Christians earning salaries significantly above the national average, but who consider it OK to pay those serving the church pathetic salaries so as to avoid altering their lifestyle too much.

A church I once belonged to was holding a meeting to discuss having a minister. One of the questions asked at the meeting was 'Do we need to pay him?'

I thought, *Pay?*

Of course not. The average minister would only starve to death after about fifty days, then we could get another one. There are two advantages to that:

1 No need for church members to do without.
2 At the end of the year, the number of unemployed ministers would be reduced by about seven.

Back to our friends...

These friends calculate what they need to live on from their less-than-national-average salaries, then give the rest away. And this is significantly more than ten per cent.

They don't live by candlelight on floorboards, but they have settled for a simpler lifestyle than they could have had.

12 GOD KNOWS BEST

Man complains to the stewardess on an international airline that the black woman sitting next to him smells. Could she do anything about it? Stewardess makes enquiries and returns. 'Yes, sir,' she says, 'there is a spare seat in first class.' And she takes the lady to her new seat.

The Bible is generally regarded as a book of 'Don't do this, don't go there, don't say that, and definitely don't speak to *them*'. Top of the pile in promoting this view is obviously the Ten Commandments which just demonstrate that God has no fun and God is going to make sure that we don't either.

Much as we don't like to admit it, we all need rules to live by. We benefit from these rules most of the time and try to beat them some of the time, but without them there would be no way of making society work.

We used to live in a house where the bedrooms were on the first floor. The window in the children's bedroom was particularly low and fully openable. It would have been quite easy for them to jump out, so we had a rule that there was to be no jumping out of the bedroom window, which was reinforced with a safety rail that I installed. The children felt we were restricting their freedom and preventing them from becoming the stunt persons of the future. But Sue and I thought it was a good rule. Can you imagine what would happen if, one morning, we came out of our kitchen door and there was Vicky splattered all over the patio? We scrape her up, put her in the back of the car and take her up to Accident and Emergency. We walk in, slap her down on the table, and the doc says, 'What's that?'

'That's Vicky,' we reply.

'What happened to *her*?' asks the doc.

'She jumped out of the bedroom window,' we say.

'How come she was able to do that?' asks the doc.

'Well, we don't like to restrict the free spirits of our children, so we did nothing to stop it and never told her she shouldn't.'

Our life as parents, I think, would be somewhat curtailed as social services step in and do what we all expect them to.

Now potentially we could argue that obviously children need rules because they don't know any better, but do we?

If there were no rule that stealing is wrong, you could go out and spend £2,000 on a music system. The neighbour hears it (as they are bound to do with a £2,000 system); neighbour thinks, *That's nice*, huzzes a brick through the window and takes it. There's no rule not to steal, so that's fine.

You and a few friends book two weeks in a luxury villa in Ibiza, sort out first-class flights, hire a Merc from the airport and look forward to the holiday of a lifetime. You pack your sun cream, swim gear, white tops and snorkel, and off you go.

You get to the airport, book in and spend loads of money in the airport lounge because there is nothing else to do. Get on the aeroplane; get to your seats – and they're occupied. 'Sorry, mate, we've nicked them. Nothing against that, is there?'

You travel to Ibiza sitting on the wing.

You get out of the aeroplane (or off it, in your case), rush to reach baggage reclaim first – then wait there till the end because your bag is the last off. Go to pick up the keys to the brand new, air-conditioned Merc sitting at the end of row E. Just as you get there, you see this brand new, air-conditioned Merc driving off. As it speeds by, the driver shouts, 'Sorry, mate, we've nicked it. Here are the keys to the 2CV we hired.'

Two days later you get to the luxury villa. Guess what? There's a brand new, air-conditioned Merc sitting outside it...

To cut a long story short, you set up a tent on the beach, open your bag and the baggage handlers have nicked your snorkel.

The Ten Commandments should be seen as ten guidelines for life rather than a set of rules to prevent fun. We ignore them and we face the consequences.

We make money our god and we become frustrated.

We misuse the name of God or displease him – who cares?

We work seven days a week and we burn out.

We ignore our parents and we learn life the hard way.

We kill and we have to explain it to the deceased's relatives – who trusts us again?

We commit adultery and the unadulterated get hurt. Who knows what happens to the children? Who trusts us again?

We steal and we end up with two snorkels.

We lie – who trusts us again?

We drool over what everybody else has and forget what we have.

Call me an old traditionalist, but if God made us, then God must know the best way for his product to live; so the ten guidelines are actually the framework by which we benefit most. Although we may knock these rules, I'm not convinced I could come up with a better set that works for everyone.

The Bible is more than religion: it is a way of life which, if followed by everyone, all would benefit from.

In Leviticus, debatably the most boring book in the Bible (I think I got away with that), the writer talks about a Year of Jubilee (Lev 25:8–55). In Exodus, Moses told the people of Israel that they should work six days and rest on the seventh. In Leviticus, they are told that they should work their fields for six years and rest them on the seventh. Then, again in old Leviticus, this principle is taken further: every seven lots of the seven-year cycles, there should be a Year of Jubilee.

What is Jubilee?

According to my dictionary, it is the celebration the Jews have every fifty years.

I am somewhat mystified as to why, in the UK, we celebrated the Queen's twenty-five years of reign with a Silver Jubilee. Silver, I accept, stands for twenty-five, but jubilee does not. So why did we all have street parties and talk to neighbours we never normally talk to and wave flags and drink beer for an occasion called 'The Silver Jubilee'? It's like me celebrating my fourteenth fiftieth golden wedding anniversary.

Anyway, this is beside the point, as I'm talking about the Leviticus Jubilee when God said that every fifty years everything stops and we start all over again.

After the Israelites had left Egypt and reached the land Moses had led them to, it was divided among the families depending on the size of the family (see Joshua

13 – 21). Life in their new country, therefore, started off for the Israelites with everybody being equal. Because of human nature, and some people being good at some things and others good at other things, some of them were better business people than others. The consequence of this was that some made their land work for them and others didn't do so well. When a family got into trouble financially, the only asset they had was their land. So if they got into debt, they sold a bit. What God proposed was that every fifty years all the land which had been bought by different people had to be given back to the original owners. To you and me, this may not seem very fair, but if you think about it for long enough it does actually make sense.

If a woman sells an acre of land, but she knows that in the Jubilee Year she is going to get it back, what is she actually selling? She is selling space for another farmer to grow crops until the Jubilee Year. If there are five years to go until the Jubilee, all she is selling is the potential crop the buyer can get out of five harvests from an acre of land. She doesn't actually sell the land as such: she is really leasing it to the buyer for five years. At the end of fifty years all debts are cancelled, the land goes back to the original owners and everybody has a party.

Now admittedly, if a farmer was a bad farmer in the last fifty years it is likely that he will be a bad farmer in the next fifty years (although some learn from their mistakes), so people may get into the same difficulties as before. But the system stops the really successful ones having loads of money and getting mega-rich, and it stops the not-so-good ones getting mega-poor.

Now why do you think God set all this up? Well, I'll tell you.

Apart from the fact that he didn't want people to starve to death, which would be the ultimate outcome if the system carried on without a Jubilee, he also wanted to get across the message that they couldn't sell the land because it wasn't theirs to sell. In Leviticus (see 19:34), the Jews are described as aliens and tenants. (Aha, so maybe an alien and a midget might turn up!)

How can anybody say that they own the land?

I own a car because people got together, made it, sold it, and I bought it.

I own a piece of land because somebody sold it to me, but who did *they* buy it from. God?

Loads of people have made their fortune out of land, but who wrote the cheque to God?

There is God, sitting there somewhere, looking down at all those who have benefited from land sales and all those who are dying because of them – but nobody has paid the original landowner.

We are all aliens and tenants

As Robert Redford said in that brilliant film, the name of which I can't remember, 'There is nothing in this life that I own. I am only passing through.'

God set up a system which allowed people to live and make a living out of land that actually belonged to God. They could earn their living, they could work hard and benefit from working hard. But they must always remember that the land they were working and renting from each other was not theirs, and neither could it ever be. And it still isn't theirs today.

Every fifty years, it was as if you finished the game, folded away the board and got out a new one. This was not communism, as some may argue; it was simply a leveller, to prevent the extremes of rich and poor. It demonstrated that everyone was of equal importance to God, because God treated everyone the same and still does.

But we don't.

I am a quantity surveyor. I have worked in most aspects of quantity surveying. I now work with large subcontractors (large in terms of turnover as opposed to large in terms of 60-inch waists). The subcontractor, in my experience, does not have as high a standing on life's social-standing scale as the main contractor. In many respects, if I mentioned second-hand-car salesmen, you would know exactly what I mean: there is an image attached to both, and both are wrong.

One hot summer's day, I and the managing director of the subcontractor I was representing met with the surveying director and the contracts surveyor of the main contractor, to agree the final account on a million-pound contract. There was great tension as both sides had a view as to the value of the account. I wore my favourite Biggles tie; Bill Dit (made-up name), the managing director of the subcontractor, had cleaned his shoes. The two surveyors for the main contractors were sitting in the best seats next to the window.

The discussion started with a preliminary round of mild joking, and off we went. About an hour into the debate, which I personally thought was not going that well, Bill excused himself from the room. We all carried on. I was in full flow, giving an astounding presentation on Contract Law which, it has got to be said, was not convincing the opposition. Bill then walked back into the meeting with a cool box. He opened the lid and removed from the box four very dainty, cut-glass desert dishes, a box and a scoop. He interrupted my presentation to enquire, 'Would anybody care for some home-made strawberry ice-cream?'

Position, status, image, arguments, gone.

Terrific leveller.

God installed a leveller because God knew what greedy illegitimate people some of us are. But, as far as

I can see, the system was never implemented. There is little history to support that anybody ever celebrated Jubilee. There are a few signs that something happened, but not on the scale God intended. This is probably because (and this is total assumption) the people who had the ability to do it were the people who acquired the land, and it wasn't in their interests to make themselves poorer in order to make their neighbours richer. Today we are living with the consequences. A few have loads and loads have nothing.

The world's ten richest billionaires have one-and-a-half times more wealth than the world's forty-eight poorest nations, so Jubilee 2000* tells us.

All because greedy fingers wouldn't do as God asked.

Throughout history, the rich minority have ruled the poor majority, which ultimately lets the poor die young.

Although placed under the heading 'Black and White', South African tension was about a system introduced by white missionaries who totally misunderstood who God is and what God stands for. The consequence? A rich minority who ruled a poor majority.

Although placed under the heading 'Tribal conflict', Rwanda was actually about one group of people entering a country belonging to another group of people years ago, and ruling it for them. The consequence? A rich minority who ruled a poor majority.

Although placed under the heading 'Religion', Northern Ireland is actually about one group of people entering a country belonging to another group of people years ago, and ruling it for them. The consequence? A rich minority who ruled a poor majority (though perhaps this example is not as extreme as the others).

And this is because we ignored the guidelines God has given us.

If only we did what God said!

So what's all this got to do with us?

The West's system of keeping poor countries in debt is not only killing thousands by the day, it is also ignoring the way God wants us to live. Politicians and economists can put forward loads of arguments why clearing debt won't work and how world markets would be affected. Well, isn't it about time the pendulum swung the other way and we gave back to the poor what is rightfully theirs?

I owned a house which I rented out for five years. The tenant paid her rent on time every month.

When the tenant moved out, she had built, and I use the term advisedly, three fishponds.

The terms of our agreement were 'not to materially alter the buildings or grounds'.

Why? Because they weren't hers.

The tenant didn't sell anything; she just materially changed my garden into a giant puddle.

Was I annoyed?

Yes.

Because it wasn't the tenant's garden. She had no right to change it.

Well, the land isn't ours either. We have no right to change it and we have no right to sell it. We have no right to benefit from a system that is against what God instigated. We may not be able to beat the system, but we can try to rectify it.

If Christians don't lead the way in cancelling debt in the developing world, nobody else will. It's not in their interests.

What are you going to do? Passively benefit from the system or support the work of organisations like Jubilee 2000* and see, to some extent, God's control strings reinstated?

Note

* Jubilee 2000 is an organisation which has been established to lobby governments to have the debt burden of developing countries cancelled by the year 2000. They believe that while countries continue to make heavy interest payments, their development is being impeded. Part of Jubilee's campaign is to produce the biggest petition in the world and present it to government, to demonstrate public concern over this issue.

13 THE PROBLEM IS TOO BIG

One Flew Over the Cuckoo's Nest is a film starring Jack Nicholson, in which he is living in a home for people with learning difficulties. During the film, Nicholson struggles with the whole way everyone is controlled by the system. One night he's standing in the washroom. In the middle of the washroom floor is a huge stone-clad drinking fountain. Frustrated once again by his fellow inmates, he says to them, 'Tonight I am going down into town to watch the ball game. Anyone coming?'

Some stare in disbelief, others laugh. One brave spokesperson eventually speaks: 'And how are you going to do that then?'

Nicholson replies, 'I am going to pick up the fountain, throw it through the window and walk right out of here.'

He walks over to the fountain and practically bursts most of his blood vessels attempting to pick this monument up. After extreme effort and energy is employed, he has to give up.

Billions of pounds are needed before a substantial impact will be made on the world's poor. To turn the two billion people who are either malnourished or undernourished into pictures of health would take money that I doubt anybody has actually calculated. The numbers certainly won't fit on my calculator.

What can we realistically do?

I used to work in West London. On a normal day, I could drive home to Chelmsford in about an hour. On Friday evening I could usually bank on it taking two and half-hours. I never really understood why Fridays were so much busier. Who was going home on a Friday night who didn't go home the other nights of the week? If they didn't go home the other nights of the week, where did they go? I understand that some people live away from home during the week, but I can't imagine it would make that much difference to traffic-flow. Loads of people go home early on Fridays, so how come when we went home at the normal time there were more people on the roads? Perhaps our normal home time was others' early time.

I remember one Friday we were going away for the weekend and I promised I would be home for six o'clock. Given the normal two-and-a-half-hour journey home, I needed to leave at three-thirty. I left at five o'clock.

There was no way I was going to land anywhere near my promised time of arrival. What do I do? Sit around the office and not bother trying to go home? Or go down the pub and drink myself into oblivion so that I have no idea whether it is Friday or Saturday?

Well, I guess the above were options, but they wouldn't have done much for the intended long-term relationship I had planned for my wife and I. So, taking a tip from my boss, I got in the car at about five past five, drove up the road, then rang home and told Sue, 'I am stuck in traffic.'

You see, if I'd rung before I left the office, Sue would know that I'd left late. By ringing after I'd left the office, she was not to know that I'd hit traffic within two minutes: she'd just think that I was on the way home and things were worse than expected. I hadn't overtly lied, just bent the truth.

OK I lied, and I have confessed and repented since.

The main point is this: if I hadn't set out, even though it was five o'clock and a hopeless task, to meet my original goal of six o'clock, I would never reached home by half past seven.

Through Tearfund, in the UK, it only costs £15 per month to support a child. What can £15 per month do?

Recently, I went to visit the child sponsorship programme in Nairobi. The way the programme works is that families approach the church for sponsorship. The church assesses their application and then, depending on funds, takes the child on. The child is sent to state school, for which fees have to be paid. School uniforms and books are provided, and each child has a social worker employed by the church to oversee his or her progress. The social worker is the link between the church, the child, the school and the family. If the child isn't attending school, the social worker gets to know and can visit the child's parents to see what the reason is. The social worker also provides assistance with child care, education, family planning, and so on. The church runs a Saturday programme for the children, where they come and take part in various activities. A midday meal is provided, along with seminars for the parents on a wide range of subjects. All in all, a comprehensive package.

Tearfund carry out their entire child-support programme through an international organisation called Compassion. There are currently 25,000 children being supported by Tearfund sponsors around the world. When I visited Nairobi, I was informed that about 20,000 children were being supported there by Compassion. The demand for support, however, was ten times that number.

Thousands of children receive an education and support from the church, and have hope for the future. All for £15 per month.

£15 per month is the cost of a CD.

The choice is yours – a CD or the future of a child.

You make that decision every day of your life.

A six-year-old boy in the UK heard a Brazilian talk about slum children in Brazil. Several weeks later, he came up to the front at church and said how the man from Brazil made him feel sad, so he was organising a 'Bring and Buy' sale. Over £200 was raised because one little boy felt sorry and was prepared to do something.

We may think that there is nothing we can do. We may think that £15 per month won't change anything. We may think that a 'Bring and Buy' sale on a Saturday afternoon isn't going to change the world. But that is exactly what could happen if everybody who says that something should be done did something.

In some parts of Africa a teacher earns about £400 per year. If you consider that a teacher in this country earns, let's say, £15,000 a year. This means that £400 given in this country has the same purchasing power as £15,000 when spent in Africa. Put another way, your pound buys something like forty times in Africa what it will buy in the UK.

Actually, because costs of living differ, this isn't strictly true. But it's not far wrong either. What may seem like nothing to us can be significant money in other parts of the world.

But do we give it? Or do we keep hiding behind the fact that we can't make a difference and so we don't.

There is a hotel chain which provides en suite bathrooms complete with hair-dryers (let's face it, these days we don't consider a hotel to be a proper hotel if they don't). On the bottom of each hair-dryer is a little sticker which says, 'Don't use in the shower.' (Ah, that would explain why I could never get my hair dry. I always thought, to save time, you just did both together...) I'd guess that most people would recognise that this is an essential part of hair-drying, although the fact that the hotel put the notice there would suggest that experience tells them otherwise.

It is so obvious what is needed from us, but we still don't get it, do we? When world disasters are reported, we still have to have stickers on the bottom of our newspapers saying, 'Give.' Because, although it would seem obvious, experience tells us that this is not happening.

Another passage of the Bible I don't quite get is where Jesus says, 'If you have faith the size of mustard seed, you can say to a mountain move and it will' (Matt 17:20).

I believe in miracles. I have seen miracles in my own life. I can imagine blind people seeing. I can picture lame people walking. I know committed atheists who have become disciples. But I cannot imagine a mountain moving.

Mountains are big. We are not talking about little hills; we are talking the things Chris Bonnington dreams about sitting on top of.

Part of my problem with mountains moving is, if God put them there in the first place what do we want to go moving them around for?

I have heard explanations about shifting plates.

I have heard explanations that if you stand at Y the mountain is there, but if you stand at X the mountain is here. But we all know that this isn't what Jesus was on about.

I can't imagine mountains moving. If you can, that's fine. But if you're like me and you can't...

I was listening to somebody – who will remain nameless, because I can't remember – who posed the question, 'How do mountains move?'

My response, of course, was, 'Stupid question. They don't move.'

But he went on to say that the way a mountain moves is a shovel full at a time.

Suddenly it clicked. Of course! Although I must confess that, as a quantity surveyor, I realised possibly more than most that it would take rather a lot of shovels.

I know I am capable of picking up a shovel, and so are you. The responsibility to move mountains is on our shoulders. If we all pick up our shovels, the mountains will move.

I am convinced that there are enough resources to change the world. There is just a lack of desire to pick up shovels.

I couldn't actually give a monkey's how mountains move; I just want to *see* them move.

You can do it with your mustard-seed faith and I'll do it with my shovel. But believe me, I know that if every person capable of picking up a shovel did, we would change the world.

This is not a ridiculous statement; it only becomes ridiculous when everybody sits around and waits for others to do it.

So you want to do something?

Let me tell you more about **Game of 2 Halves.**

In the UK, loads of us play sport. For many, sport is played several times a week. Every time we play, there is a cost attached. Sometimes we have to pay for it, at other times others pay for us. But we just take it for granted that it is our right to play sport.

In other parts of the world young people do not have the opportunity to play one sport, let alone several different sports. When Dennis Pethers of Viz-A-Viz went to Uganda some years ago, one of the activities he undertook was to sit through a seminar one sunny Saturday afternoon. He got bored and came outside, to find loads of young people all sitting round a football pitch. They were bored. When he asked, 'Why is nobody playing football?', the response was simple: 'We don't have a ball.'

In Kenya, I played football with children who also had no ball. But they had plastic bags and rags and some string which they made into a ball and kicked around until such time as there was nothing left to kick.

In the UK there is so much money in sport, so much waste and so much taken for granted. In Uganda there is no money in sport, no waste and no taking anything for granted.

The concept behind **Game of 2 Halves** is that we in the UK, who play so much sport, raise money for those who have nothing to play sport with.

Of course, there is more to playing sport than having a ball. You need to be healthy, you need education, you need the whole package of life, to get on the football pitch and score goals.

Game of 2 Halves is a nationwide project of Tearfund and Viz-A-Viz in association with Christians in Sport. The purpose is to get people who are already doing sport to raise money for those who want to do it. What is so great about the project is that we are not asking you to walk hundreds of miles, or cycle up and down the country, or go without food or anything that's difficult.

All we are saying is, using what you are already doing, raise money.

This is your chance to do something. The time for feeling sorry is over. The time for thinking others should do it has passed. It's time to pick up your shovel. Together we will move mountains.

There are loads of ideas of how we can do this. If you have any you think are better, that's fine, let us know. Whatever way round, the time to be active is now. Do what you love and help others.

There is a contact address at the back of this book. Write to **Game of 2 Halves**, and you will become part of a moving mountain.

One day I was in a cab and I had an epileptic fit. I didn't know it was coming and I didn't know where I was going. The next thing I know, I'm in Hammersmith and Fulham Hospital, my shirt and briefcase lying next to me, and I feel very pukey.

The doc comes in and asks me how I am. I respond, 'I feel very pukey.'

The doctor's response is to tell me to rest awhile, and he will come and see me later.

Instantly, I realise my mistake. If I don't feel better quick the doc is going to keep me in overnight, and I definitely do not want that.

So I get out of bed, put my shirt on, have a look in my briefcase to find the book I have been reading, sit on the edge of the bed and swing my little legs to and fro.

Doc comes back. I still feel very pukey. The conversation goes like this:

Doc: You're looking better.

Me: I feel better.

Doc: Do you want to go home?

Me: Oh, that would be nice.

Doc: Yes, you're looking a lot better. I'll arrange your discharge.

Me: Great!

(Doc makes his way to the door.)

Doc: By the way, when you're feeling really well, you'll probably read your book the right way up.

You can fool some of the people some of the time but...

Don't fool yourself any longer that praying about it is enough. Pick up your shovel.

We may never see the end result of what we start, but if we never start the end result will be fairly predictable.

Remember where we started this chapter?

The closing scene from *One Flew Over The Cuckoo's Nest* shows a huge Indian inmate of Nicholson's. He goes into the washroom, picks up the fountain and throws it out of the window.

14 I DID IT MY WAY

Man who stands on top of hill
With mouth wide open and empty stomach
Waits long time for roast chicken to fly in.

I have written this book, you have read it. Fact.

You don't know me, I don't know you. Fact for 99 per cent of you (I know this, because I gave a copy to my mum).

My life totally reflects everything I have written. Fact.

Actually, you haven't got a clue whether it does or not. So here's a bit about me, and you can make up your own mind.

I started life as a baby. Then I did a degree in quantity surveying. My best friend on the course could never understand how I passed and, I've got to say, he's got a point.

As I mentioned before, I had no intention of getting married. Then I met Sue.

I was sponsored through my studies by a large international construction company. They had directors for everything. As I watched the way it worked, I was convinced that if I kept my nose to the grindstone I could become one of those directors by the age of thirty-five. That was where I was going. A nice home and, more importantly, a big car, church on Sundays and a generous donation in the collection.

Then...

Before I was even engaged to Sue, I should have seen the warning signs.

We were out for a walk in the park, as I remember, the day before New Year. Just as we are about to get back in the car (a 1978 Ford Capri 1600L with alloy wheels – you can see I was on my way to fulfilling my ambition), Sue asks me, 'Would you ever be prepared to consider leaving your career and working for the church?'

(Let's make something quite clear. You don't have to work for the church to serve God, fulfil the work of the Holy Spirit in your life and see the kingdom of God grow.)

As Sue said this, I just stared into her eyes. No, not gazed. Stared. The reason I stared was that it's a bit like someone saying, 'I love you': you can't, in response, say, 'Wanna chip?'

When somebody tells you they love you, the relationship is either going to grow from this point on because both parties feel the same, or it's going to die because both parties feel a little different. One thing for certain, it's not going to stay the same.

Sue's question was not dissimilar, in a different sort of way. I'll explain.

The true answer to the question was NO. But I also knew that as a disciple, if I was really wanting God to have control of my life, then the answer had to be YES. You see, the crucial part to the question was 'Would you be prepared...?', not 'Will you...?'

If nobody asks you a question like this, you never have to face up to the answer. So there's no problem. But, once asked the question, you do. And I knew my answer couldn't be 'Wanna chip?'

It took me three years of wrestling and arguing and all that stuff before I could honestly say that my answer was YES. The park-keeper was not happy, because the gates shut at 5pm.

Probably all of us could look back to points in our past which were turning-points. I don't have very many, but this has got to be one of them. It changed my whole perception of life, my response to God and my ambition.

Occasionally, I have told this story to groups. Once, a couple of years ago, Sue was actually in the group I was speaking to. Later on, still in this group, Sue said, 'I know Grant sees this question as a turning-point in his life, but I don't remember why I actually asked it.'

As these words sunk in, it slowly dawned on me that a question which had changed my life permanently was just a conversation filler to Sue. If only I had realised this at the time, I could now have the nice house and big car without conscience...

I jest. I wouldn't have it any other way. But it is strange that what changed my life actually meant nothing to Sue at the time.

Here's a little preach about marriage

For any of you out there who are thinking about marriage and you have somebody in mind, I think you have to ask this crucial question, 'Do you both have similar ambition for God?'

If neither of you has ambition for God, that's fine. A total waste of investment for the Holy Spirit, but fine.

If one of you has ambition for God and the other doesn't, you have big problems. You will always be fighting the desires of your partner and eventually, I would guess, your ambition will need a magnifying glass. Live in cloud-cuckoo-land if you like, but my experience tells me that, in the majority of relationships, if a person gets married without God-ambition he or she will die without it.

If both of you have vision and these are not similar, you have an even bigger problem. I appreciate God can do anything, but if one feels a commitment to working with Florida surfers and the other to feeding refugees, the relationship is going to struggle.

If you believe the right thing to do is to get married and you're praying for guidance, the above question and subsequent answer is crucial. If God is bringing you together, then you will have goals that complement each other; otherwise it ain't going to work.

In every decision Sue and I have made, we have prayed together and made the decision together. It has never been Sue's ideas and me reluctantly following, or vice versa. Without that common commitment, there would always be a reluctant partner holding the other one back from responding to God's challenge in their lives.

Enough of that

Life progressed from that point. Sue and I got married – probably the best move I have ever made. The influence Sue has had on me has transformed me into a different person. Some of those who know me might not think the result is very good, but if I had continued the way I was going it would not have been a pretty sight.

After a few years of marriage, I was getting invited to speak in loads of churches and, remarkably, getting invited back. We began to realise that people were listening to what I had to say, and I realised that I really didn't know much about the book I was speaking about. We decided that I needed to study the Bible.

The big problem with this is obviously finance. When you're married and have children, it is not easy to go without income for a couple of years and still eat. We prayed about how God might want to deal with this. After a couple of years with no progress, a friend, Roy (not a made-up name, because that's what he's called), came round. Just as he was leaving, he said, 'Ever thought about going freelance?'

I laughed, said goodbye, put the milk bottles out, kicked the cat and went to bed.

Lying in bed, it suddenly hit me. Freelance, that's the answer. I could earn more money freelance, save up and send ourselves to Bible college. Excitedly, I explained all this to Sue. Sue's response was, 'Tell me about it in the morning.'

After a couple of months praying for signs, which we received in abundance, I handed in my notice and set up in partnership with Sue. Our aim was to work for three years and then, with the money saved, go to Bible college. We had a partnership account from which we took the same salary I used to earn; the rest, we felt, belonged to God.

Within three months, as I mentioned before, I was earning so much money I figured that, if it was invested properly, we could provide for the future – not just for a few years at Bible college but way beyond. We began to pray and again asked for signs, and we started to invest in property. We still considered that the excess money belonged to God, not to ourselves; we continued to live in a three-bedroom terraced house while the money being earned was ploughed into future investment. Within a couple a years we owned, in addition to our home, an apartment in Lanzarote, a three-bedroom detached house and a plot of land with permission to build a house. The logic being that one day we would live off the rental income and earning money would become a thing of the past.

I stress that we prayed about every step, and every step we got signs, and every step we were convinced God was showing us the way ahead. Unfortunately, we made one big mistake – hundreds of little ones, but one *big* one. Being over-ambitious, instead of saving the money and buying the above property outright, we borrowed money to do it. This was at the end of the eighties. The country was about to dive-bomb into recession, obviously not foreseen by God because we never got wind of it. Interest rates soared like an eagle after breakfast and property prices plummeted like a hot-air balloon setting off round the world. Three and a half years after we had set up the partnership, I was working anything between sixty and eighty hours a week and travelling 30,000 miles a year. We had financial commitments up to our ears; we had to earn £4,000 per month just to cover our costs, let alone have money for sweeties. We were further away from going to college than we had been three and a half years previously.

These facts struck me one night in February 1992 as I drove home. On getting home, I talked it through with Sue, then we went up to the bedroom to pray. We always prayed in the bedroom because the bedroom was upstairs and consequently you could get your reply a lot quicker from God than if you were downstairs. Another added advantage of praying upstairs is that should you fall asleep (only been known a few hundred times), you won't wake up with cricked neck.

That night we prayed.

'God, we're going to college in September '93. Right now that is financially ridiculous. You know that and so do we. So sort the finance out. If you don't and we can't go in September '93, we will never mention Bible college again. Oh, Amen.'

We never told anybody our prayer. We weren't sure

if it was theologically sound. We reckoned if God knew, that was enough.

A few weeks later I was with a very good friend, travelling to work round the M25. We were talking about life, the world and the universe, and putting them all to rights in that order, when my friend said, 'I know you and Sue have been thinking about Bible college for some time. My wife and I have prayed about it. If you carried on doing some work for my business, we would pay you what you needed to live on.'

I chuckled inside because I knew that he had little idea that we needed £4,000 per month, without a sweetie allowance, and that was after tax. So in a very condescending manner I said, 'That's a very nice offer, but you have no idea the amount of money we're talking about here.'

I sat there contemplating the offer and thinking how cool it would be to do it, but knowing it couldn't happen. My friend said, 'No, you're not listening. I said we had prayed about it and the offer stands.'

Wow, that put me in my place.

I got home, talked it through with Sue and decided to go for it. We set about trying to reduce our commitments, and in September 1993 we went to Bible college.

Over the next two years, we still had tax commitments, all of which were met from gifts we received, and our M25 friends stuck to their commitment. I can't tell you where all the money came from, though much of it was through friends who were aware of our situation, but we came out of college with a few quid in the bank and all our investments neutralised.

How do you understand what happened? Some would say that we were downright irresponsible but, because we had good friends, we were saved from bankruptcy. Some would say that we were over-ambitious. Some would say that we should have seen a financial advisor. Some would say that I threw away a good career. My mother would say, 'He's always been irresponsible with money and nothing's changed.'

I'm not sure what I would say. We did pray and it did happen. But then we prayed about a lot of other things and some happened and some didn't. I think my overall conclusion would be that at first I did it my way and eventually God said, 'Now you've had a go and failed, will you trust me to do it my way?'

Bible college was a transforming experience. I found theology inspiring, invigorating and challenging. I think that I threw most of my faith into the air and put together a new understanding of God as the pieces fell back down to earth. My concern for the poor grew, and I knew that life post-Bible college was going to be committed to making a change.

Another turning-point for me was when the Rwanda crisis hit our televisions. As a family we sponsored a child called Mujwa who lived in Rwanda. We paid £15 a month for her education and we encouraged our children to pray for her every evening. We received letters from her about four times a year, which we replied to.

When the slaughter started in Rwanda, we lost touch with her for about nine months. We didn't know if she was dead or alive, although it was very likely she was dead. As I contemplated Mujwa's life and I looked at the lives of our children, I thought, *I wonder what would happen if we swapped our daughter for Mujwa. If Vicky went and lived in Rwanda and Mujwa lived in the UK, what would our response be? If that happened, would I just sit at home, send £15 a month and let the children pray, knowing that any moment now Vicky could get machetied to death.*

I knew the answer was 'No', and that if I was serious about making a difference I had to go a lot further.

I left Bible college ready to take on the world. However, I slowly discovered the world wasn't ready for me.

We moved back to our home town and our home church. Before we went away to college, Sue and I had been very involved in the church. I was on the leadership team and Sue was involved in several activities. While we were at college, the leaders wrote to say how they would invite me back into the leadership team after I settled back into church life. They soon changed their minds. One family threatened to leave if I was made a leader. As it happens, I wasn't and they did. I'm not sure what that says, although blackmail springs to mind.

I attempted to access what I was rather than what I would like to be. I think that all of life is a big training ground. There is a danger that many of us spend our lives trying to be somebody else instead of being content to be the person God made us.

So what was I? A qualified quantity surveyor? A communicator? A scratch-the-surface theologian?

I pushed several doors with Christian development charities, attempting to utilise all of the above, none of which opened. Then one day I was sitting at my desk and the phone rang. I answered it (because that's what I normally do when the phone rings) and it was a development charity with whom I had previous contact.

The caller began the conversation with the usual pleasantries and then went on to explain that he was involved in a major hospital-building programme in Zimbabwe. Could he call on my expertise?

I was ecstatic. This was what I have been patiently waiting for. At last I'm being called by God. Is Zimbabwe ready for me?

He carried on. A church in Ireland had given money specifically for a cement-mixer. He wondered if, with my contacts, I could get the best price for one.

A cement-mixer?

Did I spend five years training and a further five years in an international company and a further ten years in my own partnership dealing with multi-million-pound contracts, to end up buying a cement-mixer?

It's not that I don't think that people who buy cement-mixers don't need skills. They do, and very important people they are too. But I was expecting my experience to be used in a slightly different way. Still, who am I to argue with the call of God?

I carried out the task, and ten minutes later went back to waiting by the phone.

Another situation involved me flying to the south of France for a weekend – not exactly caring for the poor and needy, but certainly a little nearer Africa than Ireland. I went there with one of our church leaders, and had several meetings over the weekend with various people. As we flew home, the leader I had travelled with turned to me and said, 'I am really glad that you came with me this weekend.'

I thought he was going to compliment me for my sharp mind, clarity of thought and ability to speak straight and not compromise. However, he continued, 'Yes, it was so good to spend the weekend with somebody who likes cheese as much as I do. You see, my wife doesn't, and I always feel awkward about eating cheese on my own.'

I knew I must have my uses: they just weren't particularly obvious, unless I was to make my own cheese in a cement-mixer.

Then one day I met Dennis Pethers. Dennis told me that Viz-A-Viz were looking for someone to take on their projects department which had a partnership role with Tearfund. Basically, they ran a multi-media show which went into schools, universities and churches, geared to raise awareness of the needs of the developing world. If people wanted to respond, Viz-A-Viz directed them to Tearfund. Viz-A-Viz had no overseas projects and didn't intend to start any. They saw no point, given that the likes of Tearfund already had overseas projects and knew very well what they were doing. The partnership worked because Viz-A-Viz ran the show and Tearfund ran the projects.

Since then I have worked two days a week as a quantity surveyor, which is how I earn my money. The remainder of my time I work as a volunteer for Viz-A-Viz and Tearfund. About every six months I go through the loop with Sue: would I be better off working five days a week and just giving the extra three days' pay to Tearfund? One of the drawbacks is, I probably wouldn't. But, in addition to that weakness, I actually believe God is using me to stir up more interest this way than if I just contributed money. Who knows?

I have a two-fold ambition:

1 To let God speak through me to challenge the Western church about it's superficiality and conformity to the world's consumerism; to get the church to realise that one of the most significant messages of the Bible is that, as God's creation, we have a responsibility to share what God has given us.

2 To establish one hundred universities of theology throughout the developing world, with standards of education equivalent to the West.

You may ask, 'How does theological study bring good news to the 40,000 children dying every day?'

If you are not asking this question, you can skip to

the last chapter now or chuck the book away. But if you're interested...

If you think back to the story about 'the worst slum in the world' (page 57), you may remember the bit where, because the church fed children, parents became disciples, realised their much greater self-worth, worked hard and left the slum.

> If you work with hungry people so they can eat, they feel better with full stomachs.
>
> If you work with sick people and help to cure their sickness, they feel better with less sickness.
>
> If you work with people who have no clean water and help them get clean water, they feel better because they don't get so sick.
>
> If you work with people who have no education and build schools with them, they have a better chance in life because they are educated and have understanding to contribute.
>
> But if the local church does all of the above, not only do people feel better, they understand themselves better.
>
> As a consequence of understanding themselves better, they gain a whole new perspective on life.

So why do I want to open universities of theology?

Because in many parts of the developing world the church is growing, and growing rapidly. Without trained leaders, where will it go? Without leaders who understand what it really means to be a disciple, you will end up with a church that is quite content but with no cultural relevance to its community (like somewhere else I know!). I would say that, to eradicate poverty, the church has to lead the way. To do this, it needs trained leaders. We need to help feed the hungry, but we need to go further than that and create a church which is what God intended.

Is this an ambition too far? Jesus said, 'With man these things are impossible, but with God all things are possible.'

When I was small, I had a hero. His name was Bill Woodcraft (not a made-up name; he *was* my hero). He was a friend of my family and slightly older than my parents.

I think Bill was my hero because, whenever he came round to see my parents, he always took time to speak to me. I remember that he always called me 'Chum' (probably because he couldn't remember my name, but that's OK).

Bill Woodcraft used to tell this story.

One day, a man is walking along and falls off the edge of a cliff. As he falls to certain death, he is caught on a tree that is sticking out of the cliff-face. Hanging onto this tree, he calls out.

Cliff-hanger: Is anybody there?

Voice in the dark: Yes.

Cliff-hanger: Who's that?

Voice in the dark: God.

Cliff-hanger: Can you help me?

Voice in the dark: Do you trust me?

Cliff-hanger: Yes.

Voice in the dark: Let go then.

(A long pause…)

Cliff-hanger: Is anybody else there?

15 GOODBYE

One Sunday morning at 9 o'clock, I set off for church with three friends. We travelled out of Dodoma on good roads. Then slowly the roads got smaller and smaller, until they were more like tracks than roads.

I was looking forward to my first African church service. I guess we all have our preconceptions of what African church is like. Mine was of loads of people crammed into a building meant for half the number of people there, with everybody singing, laughing and dancing with rhythm and beat.

We arrived at 10 o'clock exactly and walked in (it would have been a little silly to sit outside). As we burst through the door in eager anticipation, we were met with five other people: two women sitting on a bench on the left and two men sitting on a bench on the right and a minister-type guy with religious looking clothes. Following the trend set by the locals, the two girls I was with sat on the left and we two blokes sat on the right.

I was a little disappointed.

As we began to sing, more people turned up. After about twenty minutes, there were about 150 of us in a room designed for about 100. It was all that I had hoped for. I don't know how God felt, but I was certainly happy.

Standing next to me was an African who was translating for us. In Africa, a lot of the people you meet will speak three languages: Ki Swahili, local tribal Swahili and English. Puts me to shame as I struggle with one! After about forty-five minutes, the local translator whispered in my ear:

Local translator:	I am the preacher this morning.
Me:	Oh good. Pleased to meet you.
Local translator:	I have had a word from the Lord.

Now I love that. You get preachers who prepare at home, you get some who prepare in the car. I am sure they have asked God what he wants to say, they get up with prepared notes, and it's fine. But when a preacher says he has had 'a word from the Lord', you know you're going to get something good.

Me:	That's great. I'm looking forward to listening to you.
Local translator:	The word from the Lord is, you're to preach.

Suddenly it didn't seem quite so good anymore. I felt like asking him if, along with this 'word from the Lord', he had got a set of notes – any notes would do. Discretion being the better part of something, I kept my mouth shut.

Local translator:	At the end of this song, we will go and preach.

What he meant by 'we' would go and preach is that *I* would preach and *he* would translate.

Anyway we did and, at the end of the service, a little African woman wanted to give her life to Jesus.

What happened?

A black African man of God heard God say, 'I want this white, English-speaking person standing next to you to preach.' He must have wondered what he was hearing. How could a white, foreign-speaking Westerner be a better preacher than a local African who knew the people? (And, I might add, his logic would have been dead right.) But he trusted God to work and God did. Because there is no way the little woman responded to me: she responded to the Holy Spirit's challenge on her life.

You see, we generally trust in the ability of the speaker, but our African translator trusted in the ability of God.

I was at a seminar once with a mixed bunch of people, and the person leading asked who had ever seen a dead person come back to life. The only people who put their hands up were people who came from developing countries.

We have nothing to teach a disciple from the developing world about faith. They know how to trust God. They have to. All we have in the West is resources and education. The future for both sides to benefit must be for the developing countries to send us preachers to inspire, challenge and motivate our faith. The West, in response, needs to send resources to facilitate churches in the developing world to fulfil what they believe is their call from God. The issue is not how can we help, but how can we work together. To a limited extent this partnership is already happening, but it needs to happen to a greater extent.

I listened to Joel Edwards, the President of the Evangelical Alliance, talk about the slave trade and how the Western church was an integral part of that. As he continued to speak, I wondered why that was so? Was it that the church knew it was wrong but they made a lot of money out of it so they carried on regardless? Was it that they were ignorant and only changed as radicals began to point out their mistake? Either way, today, some two or three hundred years later, the Western church would want to distance itself from such treatment of people and would be ashamed to confess our responsibility for such abuse of human rights.

As I thought about this, I wondered, *What will the Western church be ashamed of in two hundred years time, as it looks back on the way we acted in the twentieth century?*

The conclusion I came to was embarrassing. Because I think there is a lot:

Treatment of women.

Lack of significance given to children.

Inability to trust the Holy Spirit to work through new Christians.

The culture club we have turned church into.

Total disregard of the needs of the poor.

To name a few, and I'm sure you can think of more.

But it doesn't have to stay that way.

One day all of us will be answerable to God for what we have and have not done. Once we understand what needs to be done, we can't blame past generations: we have to take responsibility for our own actions.

I once saw a spoof advert for 'Environmentally friendly disinfectant'. It didn't kill 99 per cent of household germs, but it got very disappointed with them! What does that remind you of?

As I travel round different churches, I have come to the conclusion that here is one common weakness in most of them.

They lack vision.

When I say they lack vision, what do I mean?

What is the church?

The church is God's people.

When church members get angry that their church doesn't get cleaned regularly enough, what they are really saying is they can't be bothered to get off their butts and clean it. Because the church members are the church, and I doubt we need a referendum to allow somebody to spring-clean the church.

When I say lack of vision, what do I mean?

I mean that people who go to church have no concept of why they are filled with the Holy Spirit, why Jesus died for them, why they need to respond now and what God wants them to do with their lives. All most people know is that because of Jesus they are saved from hell, which is a nasty place, and as long as they can keep the numbers up in the church they have responded to God. Church meetings are more about keeping all the members happy than killing 99 per cent of household germs.

Unity unity unity unity unity...

As long as we don't lose members, the hungry can starve and the rest can go to hell.

I have preached my little heart out on occasions. Sweat has poured off me. The adrenaline has been pumping. I have dragged every part of my body into presenting the message that I hope God has given me. And what do I get?

'That was great. Loved the story about the dog. I've got a dog...'

Is it me? Or are we missing the point?

What is your vision? What is your God-ambition?

When I speak to people in the Western church and ask them how they see the long-term future for their lives, I get:

'When the children are off my hands, I'll probably get into further education.'

'I think I'm happy in this job now and will stay there till retirement.'

'I think I'll stay where I am for a couple of years and then look around.'

'Things are going well, sales are up, we are looking to new markets.'

When I ask parents how their grown-up offspring are, I get:

'They're married now, you know.'

'She's just had a promotion.'

'Unfortunately, their marriage didn't work out.'

'He's just been given a new car.'

Do I hear about the impact of the Holy Spirit in their lives?

When I go to a developing country and ask the same question I get:

'We believe God wants us to expand the children's programme so that we are feeding a thousand.'

'Our next step is to build a polytechnic to go beyond the work God is already doing.'

'I want to get more training to become a pastor.'

'We want to start a program to reach young men for Christ.'

'We want to build an auditorium to diversify God's work in the project.'

The difference is that they have already seen what God can do and they want to see God do more. Whereas the Western church is more preoccupied with supporting the system.

Of course, I generalise. There are Western disciples who have God-ambition and there are disciples in developing countries who want personal betterment. But as an overall picture, the above is no lie, in my opinion.

A project I visited in Dagoreti, Kenya, began ten years ago by helping one child get an education. Now they:

support 530 children in education;

have a child feeding programme;

have an adult training programme;

provide education in craft skills;

want to establish a polytechnic for practical training;

plan to have workshops for training and self-support;

plan to build an 800-seater church.

And these plans are for the next few years, not wild, aimless ambitions that might happen within their lifetime.

What am I going to do?

We look at Jonah and laugh at his disobedience to God, but at least he *did* something. As Forest Gump said, 'You stand a much greater chance of winning the lottery if you buy a ticket.' I don't support the lottery, OK, but at least if you try, two things might happen:

Something or nothing.

If you do nothing, one thing will happen!

I have never understood how a fax machine works. You feed a piece of paper into a tiny slot and thousands of miles away somebody is seeing exactly what you are seeing. You can be taking hold of the top of the piece of paper and that person thousands of miles away will be reading the bottom.

If you look at the back of a fax machine, you will see one tiny cable disappearing into the wall. That piece of cable must be connected to other cables which cover the world like a big grid, and I am at the end of it. What happens when it gets to the sea? Are there loads of cables floating about in the ocean? If there are as many as there must be, why don't fisherman utilise them? I don't understand.

Now, I am told, all I need is a mobile phone, a laptop, a modem and a car, and I can go sit in the middle of a field and send thousand-page documents round the world in seconds. No cables, nothing. Do you understand that?

I can't even cope with how a mobile phone works. I can understand a mobile phone connecting with a landline phone, but two mobile phones connecting with each other while you are both moving around I just don't get. I would have thought you'd get the conversations of loads of different people.

Even though the technology has been explained to me and I can grasp the academics, I still don't understand the reality. But I use fax machines, I use mobile phones, I send e-mails and I'm building up to sitting in the middle of a field one day.

I don't understand how God works either, but my experience has been that when you take a risk with God, sometimes it works and sometimes it doesn't.

This is potentially the most significant statement I have made, which I appreciate doesn't seem to be that profound, but I am sick of people telling one side of the story. The truth is that sometimes God works miracles and sometimes God doesn't. I guess if there were always miracles, there would be no miracles, because they wouldn't be miracles anymore – they would be normal and thus require no faith.

The reality of my life is that there have been some great big failures and a couple of significant successes, but I would rather die having tried and failed and tried and succeeded than never to have tried at all.

I was talking to a church leader recently, whose name is Gwinderlin (made-up name to protect my life). Gwinderlin is a person who has my greatest respect. Gwinderlin sits at the top of the pile of a successful national company. Having spent some time with Gwinderlin, I also have an idea about her views in respect of the direction the church should be going in and what would happen if she were at the top of the pile in the church leadership too. But I see little of Gwinderlin's influence in the decisions made by the leadership team, so I asked Gwinderlin why.

Me: Why is that you are responsible for a large multimillion-pound, profitable national company, which must mean that you're a woman of great determination and influence, but so little of your influence is apparent in the decisions the church make?

Gwiny: I think it's because I spend so much time battling at work that by the time I come to leadership team meetings I'm done in.

Me: Isn't that a shame? Wouldn't it be terrific if you spent so much time battling at leadership team meetings, that by the time you got to work you were all done in?

I don't have a problem with disciples being the chairpersons of large companies. I don't have a problem with disciples wanting to be the chairpersons of large companies. I don't have a problem with disciples earning large amounts of money. I don't have a problem with disciples *wanting* to study for good qualifications. I don't have a problem with ambition.

But my question is, 'Is your ambition for God or for you?'

We were born to achieve. We get satisfaction from achievement – that is the way God made us – but who are we achieving for? And does it make any difference to how we, who say we are saved from hell because of Jesus, channel our achievement?

Are your ambition, career and position in life going to facilitate your service for God, or are your ambition, career and position in life going to be goals in themselves?

Are you going to build God's kingdom on earth as it will be built in heaven, or are you going to build your own little kingdom here?

How does Jesus dying for you and the gift of the Holy Spirit make you different from your neighbour?

Does Jesus really mean everything to you, or is he just the subject of nice songs you sing on Sundays?

In case you haven't realised, this book is about helping you realise that there is a world of poverty out there, some of which is on your doorstep and some of which is the other side of the globe. Are you going to do anything about it?

I have a little confession. A bit late I know but, even so, worth owning up to. I want to see more people motivated to working with poverty, but if this book motivates you to start a Christian business with real Jesus ethics, which impacts the community for Jesus rather than just making mega-bucks, then I'm happy with that too.

I believe that, with the Holy Spirit, we can make

impact, we can move mountains, we can change the world. **Game of 2 Halves** is a start. Write off for information now and make a difference. But it is only that – a start.

In *Strangers to Neighbours*, David Evans writes:

> *Many Christians don't realise the difference they can make. Others would be very willing to help if there was something for them to do, but I don't think there are enough visionary people putting projects together in which Christians can get involved.*

Why aren't there visionaries?

Because we expect so little from God.

In 1997, a man of eighty-seven ran the marathon. Another man of sixty ran it three times (on the same day). All that energy, but for what?

I was listening to one of the students who had been on a task force team with Tearfund. He spoke in a church about visiting a slum, going into people's houses and seeing their living conditions. He spoke about the streams of sewage running through the streets and the shoeless children running through those streets. He spoke of the despair and the hunger and the sickness. He spoke about being invited to a home in the slum. The home consisted of a couple of rooms, very dark, very hot and very crowded.

While there, it was brought to the team's attention that one of the children of the family was sick. As the team had gone in with the local pastor, the pastor asked if one of them would like to pray for the child. But before they prayed, could somebody from the team just give this mother a word of encouragement?

There was some hesitation, as you can imagine. What do you say to a woman who has no husband, who has no money, who has a sick child, who lives in a slum, who has no job, who has little prospect of changing her situation?

'Jesus loves you'?

I don't think so.

Given these conditions, it was difficult to come up with a comment on the spur of the moment. But somebody did. This is what I am told was said, 'Tell this lady that back in the UK we are doing everything we possibly can to help.'

The student hesitated at this point in the story as the reality of what had been said struck home. Because, as he gave his report in the church, everybody knew that the statement was a lie. They knew it was a lie because if we were doing everything we possibly could in the UK, then we wouldn't have the lifestyle we have and the woman in question wouldn't be living as she was either.

The student then went on to say this: 'One day I want to go back and see that lady again. I want to go back and tell her that when I visited her home in 1998 we lied to her. But now things have changed and that statement is now true.'

The only way he is going to be able to do this is if the UK church is stood on its head. The only way the church will get stood on its head is if you put it there. But while you support a two-tier system of 'what's mine is mine and what you haven't got is your problem – but don't worry, I'm praying about it', the hungry will continue to starve, the sick will continue to die, the homeless will have no home, and you and I will have to explain why to God.

There is a verse in the Bible which says, 'Faith without action is dead' (James 2:26).

Now, generally, if we understand the Greek and you dig about into original meanings, you can find out that what was written years ago doesn't actually mean what it appears to mean. So I have attempted to find out what the word 'dead' means in the original text. My conclusion is that 'dead' is rather a strong way of putting it: 'without any life' would be more comfortable perhaps.

However, 'without life' could suggest 'sluggish' or 'lifeless', which is not really an adequate description. The conclusion I come to, therefore, is that probably the best way to describe the word 'dead' is the word 'dead'.

How is your faith?

Sick? Sleeping? Not feeling too well? Lifeless? Or just plain dead?

At it's simplest level, we have loads and loads of nothing if faith has no action.

It's time the pendulum swung.

EPILOGUE

when love is a myth that others lied
a shallow gesture, the illusive prize
and self-respect's a play that I've no part in
confidence a gloss that I pretend to bask in
when uganda and sudan are headlines of profanity
governments cry shame in their pseudo-ridden morality
beggars embarrass belfast outside the doors of waterstone's
and CDEs aspire to be shallow AB1s
why is God unmoved and voiceless
a father figure who never loved us
a deity devoid of care
a heavenly being who left us here
why is God the last resort of all
the one we want to solve it all
when in fact He should be named and shamed
for the way He's let us take the blame
why do pastors tell me not to question
have faith, take heart, it's beyond your comprehension
why don't they tell me where it's really at
the bloody truth He's been getting at
that He too sweated in humanity's cesspit
went through it all, endured this shit
endured our pain, our blame, our shame
and lost the dice in nature's game

why don't they tell me it breaks His heart
to see our pain, our fear, our crap
to watch while africa is slaughtered
on the crucifix of capitalist altars
why don't they tell me we've ballsed it up
it's not His fault we lost the plot
why don't they tell me I've played my part
in wimping out and breaking hearts
why? cos no one wants to take the blame
for inflicting hurt and ignoring pain
we've renamed justice what's right for me
and paraded rights not responsibility
the pastors sell their shallow comfort
but religion masks the message God sent
He spelled it out in Jesus' name
we ballsed it up, He took the blame
so when loneliness reaps the seeds we sow
and africa starves while our souls implode
God lives our pain, our crap, our fear
we missed the point when He was here

(Rosie Uffindell)

CAN YOU KICK IT?

If you would like to find out more about **Game of 2 Halves**, then cut out this page and send it to:

Game of 2 Halves, PO Box 5895, Bentalls, Basildon, SS12 3GP.

Name ....

Address ....

....

....

....

....

....

Postcode ....

Daytime telephone no...

Date of birth ....

Game of 2 Halves is a project of Tearfund and Viz-A-Viz in associaton with Christians in Sport.